To Barbara,
Su

Connie Sharkey

ABOUT THE COVER

The empty cross and the butterfly are both symbols of the Resurrection and newness of life.

Cover design by the author

ISBN

Westview
Publishing, Inc.
8120 Sawyer Brown Road, Suite 107
Nashville, Tennessee 37221
(615) 646-6131
http://www.westviewpublishing.com

PROLOGUE AND ACKNOWLEDGMENTS

I am indebted to many who influenced the writing of this book. God urged me to write it and I love Him dearly and the wonderful family He has given me. To every person mentioned in "HE GIVES US HOPE," I am grateful for touching my life and for what they have contributed.

This book didn't "just get written," it evolved. In the evolutionary process there were some who gave generously of their gifts and time. In its first form Margaret Watson of Nashville typed the manuscript. Then I asked Charlie Winters, who was Shark's professor of Theology at Sewanee, to read it for its theological content. I wanted that to be "checked out" so that I wouldn't inadvertently say something heretical; since I have learned through prayer, study, the Bible, other people, and life as a homemaker, and not through a seminary curriculum. In Nashville, one of the members of my prayer group, Suzanne Brunson, who said she was a journalism major, offered to edit it for me, and did so. When I began making revisions, I did the typing myself which, by the way, took me longer to type than to write! Years later, after another revision, Dr. Susan Seyfarth, a parishioner in Cedar Key, Florida, graciously edited it for style. And then when I found that another parishioner, Bruce Young, had written and published a book on editing, he went over it and called to my attention typographical and spelling errors. Bruce said I didn't use many commas and that the reader's understanding might be enhanced if I used more. I added a lot more and may not even be consistent but– after all–who cares? This is for friends!

So many people have prayed me through this and encouraged me to make it available, and I thank every one of them, including my dear husband Shark, and my loving children, who made it possible in this form.

I'd like to thank Bonnie Moore of Nashville who offered to type and proofread the book after I had made some corrections and additions, and Jane Weiland for formatting the book. Thank you, also, to Hugh Daniel and Paula Winters for their help at Westview Publishing.

I hope you like "HE GIVES US HOPE" and it speaks to you. That's what God and I want.

TABLE OF CONTENTS

Page

Chapter 1
WHO NEEDS HOPE?

Why did you pick up this book? Because you are dejected? I was too. Are you disappointed in what is happening to your life? Have your dreams gone down the drain? Are those sparkling joys you were sure were ahead of you vanishing in thin air?

Are you bored? After you have acquired them, have you found that the clothes, cars, boat, house, or position you felt sure would make you happy for life are not the answer?

First of all, let me give you an exciting little gem of information. You are not a bit different from most of us. There may be a few lofty souls who have stayed above all that. I am sure there are and my hat is off to them, but I am not one of them.

You probably are not getting out of balance or going off your trolley. This may be the beginning of your gaining honest to goodness, very real deep-down stability.

Some people may envy those who have never been in such a state of affairs. I do not. I am glad I have been in those sets of circumstances because I know the difference, the before and after feeling.

I know that I have been dejected, disillusioned, disappointed, bored, and still get down in the dumps occasionally, but now I know a secret, a joyous one, the way out of such a dilemma. It is so exciting I would like to pass it on to you.

The prerequisite for getting out of your predicament is being in it! One has to be dissatisfied before one desires something better.

Did you ever realize that your problem could be something positive? It can be a real opportunity. Think of that!

I can speak from experience because I have had a very distinct change in my life. We all have changes as the years go by with growing up, which is an ongoing process and hopefully never ends, we all have lots more to learn. We have transitions from school to career or vocation; from being single to being married; with the growth of our families as our children come into existence; as we experience joys, sorrows, failures, successes, illnesses, and healing.

Probably less, rather than more of the population today, live their entire lives in the locale of their birth; therefore the majority of us have had some upheavals and transplantations into new environments where we must put down roots and blossom in new gardens. We glean wisdom and understanding and often deep joy from those who touch our lives, from our interpersonal relationships. I have been richly blessed by the opportunity of being part of a mobile society. I rejoice in the fact that there are many beautiful souls with whom my life has been intertwined. My garden of friendship is diverse and magnificent.

I believe that in every close relationship each person derives an added gift from the other and that the reciprocal giving enriches and enlarges our personalities.

Because I have been so richly blessed as the wife of an Episcopal priest for the past forty-one years, I wish to share some of the interesting experiences that led up to our call, and the tremendous changes and glorious life we have known in the ministry.

Naturally, the ordained ministry is not for everyone. My husband was called to that particular vocation by Almighty God and has pursued it joyfully. I was called by God to a real ministry but have never had the call, the desire, or the training to be ordained. My ministry has been equally joyful.

When we listen to God, who created us and gave us the gifts we possess, and follow the guidance He gives us by speaking directly to us, through others, or through circumstances, we are often enabled to find our niches.

We have differing skills, environments, personalities, and responsibilities and it is not always easy to find out just what we are meant to be or do; but when we do attempt to discover that for which we are best suited and then are willing to get out of the ruts we are in and venture into new paths, we can really begin to LIVE.

I know a number of people whose lives attest to the truth of those statements. They are genuinely happy people.

Fred, a friend we knew quite a number of years ago in Norris, Tennessee, was one such person. He changed from a job that was rather humdrum for him, that of checking out patents, to a much more challenging one which utilized his creativity and his beautiful command of language, that of writing patents. Seldom have I seen such a change come over a person. Not only was he happier, but his whole family appeared to be also.

We knew Fred in our church. A lot of people were praying for him and I saw a marvelous example of the results of prayer. Intercessory prayer was new to me, in fact I was still on the fringe, just beginning to get interested and I witnessed something very beautiful.

Fred and his wife, Dorothy, and our Episcopal priest, Hank, and his wife, Faye, were praying for my husband, Shark, and me, too.

It is interesting to me that the prayers of others seem to be more effective for us than those we pray for ourselves. It is likely due to the fact that we often slant ours in the direction of what we think we ought to do, which might not be at all what would be best for us.

When we are entwined in a difficult situation and unable to see clearly and do not have a sense of direction, the prayers of friends are ever so helpful. In fact, the prayers of those we have never met carry tremendous power. It is a beautiful mystery.

Much of God is mystery. I am so grateful because if we could understand all about God, He would not be a God to worship and adore.

I will tell you some of how Shark's and my experiences evolved. Of course I must relate them from my own perspective because one can only honestly talk about his or her own feelings even though an entire family is involved.

God has influenced our lives in most unexpected ways and has been leading us in a really exciting and beautiful life.

We never know exactly what we are going to do next or where God will lead us, but because of His love we have known, and the situations He has led us through, we know that we can trust Him implicitly. We rest assured that He will be with us always.

My husband, the Reverend William Lawrence Sharkey, an Episcopal priest, was born in 1921 and raised in Trenton, New Jersey.

His father, Samuel Miller Sharkey, raised in Boston, was educated to be a ceramic engineer. While working at his job by day and attending school and studying diligently by night he became what he really wanted to be, a Certified Public Accountant, even teaching night classes at his alma mater, Rutgers University. "Pop's" transition from being an engineer in the family business of manufacturing ceramic door knobs to being a CPA, in which capacity he utilized his innate ability for working with numbers, is another aspect of the positive effect of changing vocations. He worked at his chosen profession until he had a stroke in his eighties.

"Nana," nee Ernestine Lawrence Robbins, was from Philadelphia. After graduating from Smith College, she married Sam Sharkey, and along with raising their three sons, Sam, Hank, and Bill, she did substitute teaching and volunteer hospital work. "Tina" was an avid bridge player and was in more than one bridge club. She was also an excellent knitter and created many items for friends and acquaintances on commission.

They lived in a charming house in the country, outside of Trenton.

I was born Mary Constance Griffith in 1922, and raised in Cincinnati, Ohio.

My daddy, Thomas Herman Griffith, was a major league baseball player until I was three years old. He played for thirteen years in the National League in the same era as Babe Ruth and Ty Cobb. Tommy Griffith played with the Boston Braves in 1913, the Cincinnati Reds from 1915-1918, the Brooklyn Dodgers from 1919-1925, and the Chicago Cubs in 1925. He was with the Dodgers when they played in the World Series in 1920.

Along with his baseball career, Daddy wrote and published a number of songs, and teamed up with "Rabbit" Maranville, another famous baseball player, to play vaudeville circuits for a season or so.

When he retired from baseball, he owned and operated three radio and sporting goods stores that bore his name, in the city of Cincinnati, until he lost them in the depression.

Daddy was able to get a job as a deputy clerk, in the Hamilton County Common Pleas Court and the Domestic Relations Court, to provide some income. He then went with the W. E. Lord Insurance Company. When he became proficient in insurance, he started his own company, the Tommy Griffith Insurance Agency, which he

4   He Gives Us Hope

operated until his death.

My mother, nee Lisette ("Dette") Louise Bidenharn, born in Somerton, Ohio, went to Mt. De Chantel boarding school in Wheeling, West Virginia, near her home and then was trained for work with the deaf at the Clarke School for the deaf in Northampton, Massachusetts. She taught deaf people to lip read and to speak. When my two sisters, Fran and Peg, and I were growing up, mother was a housewife and an avid gardener. She dearly loved flowers and had beautiful gardens. She was an excellent bridge player and taught bridge classes in our home. She also had quite a bit of artistic talent.

Shark's childhood was a happy one though plagued with asthma and hay fever. Because of his allergies, he spent many summers when he was young with his maternal grandmother on Great Chebeague Island in Casco Bay, Maine. He dearly loved being there. With crowded classrooms and consequent dust problems in the public schools, he changed to a private school, and then for his high school years went to George School, a Quaker preparatory school in Bucks County, Pennsylvania. That was a very rewarding experience, and it was while he was there that Shark took up tennis which was his love for years. He caddied and played golf in Maine. My husband is a real sports fan.

The Griffith girls, of whom I was the youngest, had lots of fun as we lived next door to a suburban park. We were blessed with tennis courts, swimming pools, softball games, and plenty of green grass where we hit golf balls, romped in the summer, and went sledding in the winter. We had all kinds of athletic equipment from daddy's stores, including golf clubs, tennis rackets, bows and arrows, and bicycles for outdoors, and a ping pong table, gymnastic rings and bars with a mat on the floor in our basement for indoor activities.

The depression made its impact on me during my youth since daddy lost his business. We had a real financial struggle during my teens.

My education was in the Cincinnati public schools. The grammar school was within walking distance and we went to Withrow High School on the street car.

When college time came I entered the Teacher's College at the University of Cincinnati preparing to be a kindergarten-primary teacher. Again I commuted by street car and was fortunate to obtain scholarships for my tuition. I joined the Delta Delta Delta sorority.

Shark gravitated to the south to the University of North Carolina where he joined the Beta Theta Pi fraternity and was on the tennis team. He was also in the Naval R.O.T.C.

My first extended time away from home was as a counselor at Camp Sequoia, a private camp for girls in Bristol, Virginia. I was also gradually gravitating southward.

After my third year in college at U.C., and during my third summer at camp, I received a phone call that really changed the course of my life.

The Tri Delta national rushing chairman asked me if I would go to the University of North Carolina, all expenses paid including books and travel, to help start a chapter of the sorority there. She had checked with my parents and they had given their consent. The decision was up to me.

After thorough investigation about degrees offered, and credits, I decided that, even though the University of North Carolina did not offer a teaching degree, I would accept the generous offer and attend Chapel Hill for one year, for the new experiences of going away to college and helping start the new chapter, and then return to U.C. to finish there.

In the fall of 1943 my parents, my sisters, and a number of Tri Delt friends from U.C. bade me bon voyage at the train station. I was bound for Chapel Hill. That was a memorable year.

I loved living in the Tri Delt house and getting to know the fifteen girls who were also there for the adventure; and I met a very special lady, our housemother, Mrs. E. Merlin Schenck (lovingly called "Fifi" by her own daughters and her Tri Delt daughters) who took me under her wing and gave me lots of much-needed maternal love. Fifi had formerly been the Beta housemother and played cupid in introducing me to Shark.

We met in November, were engaged in December, and married in February. We really fell in love and had a whirlwind courtship.

He Gives Us Hope

Suddenly the Navy had needed deck officers and in February of 1944, Shark's class had been pulled out of school and commissioned.

We had been planning on being married in Cincinnati in June after Shark's graduation; but since his matriculation was altered and we didn't know where he would be in June, we decided to get married in Chapel Hill at the Tri Delt house where our mutual friends were. During war time gas coupons for driving were hard to come by, consequently few of those friends would have been able to come to Cincinnati.

On February 25th, Shark became Ensign William Lawrence Sharkey and the next day I became his wife. We were deliriously happy.

He was assigned duty at the Sub Chaser Training Center in Miami, Florida, where I was with him for three months. From there Shark was assigned to Sub Chaser 646 operating in the Gulf and Caribbean. We lived part of the time in Miami and part in Key West. When the 646 went out to the Pacific, I went home to get a job and be with my family.

The rest of World War II we were apart, as the 646 was eventually sent to Alaska where she was turned over to the Russians on the lend-lease program. After leave, Shark spent the remainder of his Naval career on the P.C.E.R. 848 in the Pacific, entering Tokyo Bay shortly after the Peace Treaty was signed.

When he had served his required time in the Navy, Shark came home and he began searching for a job. We looked in Trenton, Cincinnati, Philadelphia and environs to no avail, and then headed down south again. Finally, we decided that Shark should go back to Chapel Hill and finish his degree. He had one more year.

While Shark was at school, I got a job teaching in a private nursery school, in fact I was the director.

That fall, I became pregnant. We had not yet planned to start our family, but we were excited. We had been married a little more than two years. The baby was due in June.

We lived in a little house in the country outside Chapel Hill in a beautiful setting. I had a very good pregnancy with no complications and we were joyfully anticipating Shark's graduation from college, a job somewhere, and a baby to love.

In June, shortly after graduation, which was really a milestone for us, the time came for me to deliver. We drove miles to Duke Hospital in Durham, had trouble getting in because the hospital had been plagued by a pyromaniac and had tight security on the doors, most were locked. We finally got in the emergency entrance and after thirty-six long hours of labor, I was delivered of a five and a half pound baby girl. She had a birth defect in her back, spinal cord and nervous system, spina bifida.

The doctors informed Shark that she could not live long and they discussed when to tell me. He said they must tell me the truth immediately.

What a blow, what a shock! You wait patiently and eagerly for

He Gives Us Hope

nine months and then wham, you're hit like a ton of bricks!

At that time we did not attend any church. We were not connected with any Christian groups. We weren't thinking about God at all. We were going our own way. We must have turned to God momentarily, I'm sure we did. Most people turn to Him sometime when they are in real trouble. God did not ignore us. He was there and He helped and comforted us.

It was an unusual experience and lives indelibly in my memory. The doctors had advised me not to see the baby, to leave her in the hospital to be cared for, and go home. To do that was the most difficult decision I had ever had to make. We found out later that the doctor had a sister who had been an invalid all her life. The strain on his mother had been very hard, hence the doctor's advice to me.

On the fourth day I was waiting for Shark to come and get me. I was in the room with three other women who all had their babies brought to them regularly. That nearly killed me.

Some way, some how (and I know now that it was the Holy Spirit speaking to me), I knew that I should have our baby baptized. The strange part was that I did not even know the full significance of baptism. I just knew I should have it done.

I asked to go into a private room where I could have the use of the phone. So I went across the hall, found a phone, and called a Presbyterian minister whose name I got out of the phone book. I told him the situation and asked if he could come that day. He said he would be glad to and came shortly thereafter and administered the sacrament of baptism to our baby. Neither Shark nor I were present. Sally Robbins Sharkey was made a child of God and an inheritor of the Kingdom of Heaven.

About that time Shark arrived at the hospital. I had been unable to tell him what I was doing because we had no phone at our little house in the country. I informed him quickly of the turn of events, he met the minister, who then came into see me. We thanked him profusely and the man left.

While all that was going on, unbeknownst to me, one of the girls who shared the room with me had been aware of what I was doing and had told one of the nurses who in turn had informed the head nursery nurse.

They must have been very perceptive and wonderfully sensitive Christians. I will always be grateful for all who were involved and to God for touching their hearts and ours, because shortly after Sally was baptized, God took her into His everlasting safekeeping forever. The head nursery nurse had known she was about to die and had kept her under oxygen until the minister arrived and baptized her. She came from God and was returned to God.

We gave her body to Duke Hospital for research and I am grateful to say that in the ensuing years tremendous strides have been made in the treatment of babies with birth defects.

At our family burial plot we have a marker with the following inscription: Sally Robbins Sharkey, June 29, 1947 – July 3, 1947, "In her short span she still did serve her fellow man, Body given for research."

We gathered up my things and left the hospital with deep sadness but also a feeling of peace. God can reach those who have been ignoring Him. He is merciful, compassionate, and loving, and much more ready to give than we are to receive. His mercy and overriding care do not stop after the trauma of a shocking experience in our lives. God fills voids if we let Him. He never closes one door that He does not open another.

Shark was hired by Parker Pen Company as a salesman and tried that job for a while. It was not entirely satisfactory and so he put out feelers for different job opportunities, while continuing to work for Parker Pen.

As for me, having been psychologically and emotionally prepared to care for a child, a strange and unexpected situation arose where I feel sure God again intervened.

A close friend of ours, Bill Morgan, a doctor who had once saved Shark's life when he had suffered a bad attack of asthma with complications while in college, called and asked if we could possibly do him a huge favor. His wife was ill and in the hospital for a prolonged period of time, and he needed someone to move in and "hold his home together" as he put, while his wife was away. He had a seven-year-old daughter, Neal, at home. Their very young son was staying with his grandparents.

We would have done about anything for Bill, we were so grateful, and so we moved in and I took care of Neal and the running of his household, plus taking a course or two at the University.

Shark worked and I was busy and so did not have time to dwell on my own problems. The void in my life was filled temporarily as well as the doctor's immediate need with that arrangement, and Shark did not have to worry about me when he had to go out of town.

Shortly after we moved in, Shark was offered a job with Thornton Sales Service, a company based in Greensboro, North Carolina. He was very interested in the firm and when Mr. Thornton offered him the territory of middle and eastern Tennessee, and a small portion of North Carolina, he decided to take it and try it out. We felt that while I was safely situated in the Morgan household Shark would be free to see how he liked the new selling job as a manufacturer's representative.

I was at Bill's for nine months and Shark really liked his new occupation. He came home every weekend and on holidays. Bill told me so much about his wife whom he adored. It helped him to talk.

Human beings are in this world to help one another.

The twenty-third Psalm says in one part, "Yea though I walk through the valley of the shadow of death I will fear no evil for Thou art with me, Thy rod and Thy staff they comfort me." Notice that it does not say "up to" but "through" the valley. God never leaves us. We may leave Him, but He is always there with outstretched arms to take our hands in His and lead us wherever we go, no matter what we have to go through. He promised.

Death is a part of life. It is not something to be afraid of for ourselves or our loved ones. Jesus Christ Himself has been there and sanctified it and through His Resurrection and Ascension has given us the victory.

Chapter 2
SOMETHING WAS MISSING

I had never been to Tennessee and really didn't think I would like it. My only image was of hillbillies with pointed hats, smoking corn cob pipes, sitting on mountain tops. Little did I know what beauty I was about to behold.

Thanksgiving 1947 I had my first glimpse of east Tennessee when Shark, who was very pleased with his job, took me to Knoxville.

The arrangement that Mr. Thornton had made with Shark was that we could live anywhere in the vicinity of Knoxville which was about the center of Shark's territory.

Pam Hotard, a Tri Delt we knew in Chapel Hill, had married Ted Schulze from Tennessee. When they had found out that we would be moving to that state and that we at that time preferred living in small towns near cities rather than in the cities, Ted said to be sure to visit Norris where he had come from.

We did just that and fell in love with the beautiful little town. It was charming.

Norris was owned by TVA and was designed for those who were building the first dam of the Tennessee Valley Authority system. It had expanded since its inception but was still quaint.

The streets follow the contour of the countryside up and down through the hills and valleys. Dogwood, redbud, and pine trees are everywhere along with many other varieties of beautiful flowers. Flowering shrubs and lovely flowers grow in profusion. It is truly picturesque.

That was it. That was where we wanted to live.

In January of 1948 we moved to Norris, Tennessee, to begin the next phase of our lives together.

We happened to be the first couple to be allowed to move into the town who were not in any way connected with TVA. Restrictions had just been lifted.

We lived first in a one bedroom apartment then later moved into a different one with three rooms, two downstairs and one up.

He Gives Us Hope

I worked for TVA in the Forestry Department as a file clerk, mail girl (delivering mail to the various departments), and as emergency switchboard operator. The latter was quite an experience.

I wanted a job that did not require any training and one that I could leave at any time and not cause rehiring problems for the department. Then another milestone occurred in our lives.

The town of Norris was sold by TVA to a private corporation and homes were available for sale. In that time frame we were excited in the discovery that I was again pregnant. We had felt that we were settled enough to once again try to have a family. The doctors had assured me that there was no reason that I could not have more children and that they would very likely be normal and healthy.

A marvelous obstetrician, Dr. Lou Hefley, in Knoxville, took very special care of me after we informed her of our previous experience with Sally. We were anticipating with very positive feelings the birth of our second child.

We also wanted to put down roots and purchased the one and only home we have ever owned.

It was darling. White brick with green shutters, in a pine and dogwood setting, with a good sized grassy back yard which descended by terraces, that Shark and I developed, down into a woods below.

There was room for our eventual vegetable garden on the terraces and rambler roses along a fence in the corner of the yard.

A patio where we could sit and enjoy the outdoors and have a little rubber pool for toddlers was behind one back porch. Behind the other, back off the kitchen, we later put in a sandbox, swing, and jungle gym. It was a perfect setting for a young family.

William Lawrence Sharkey, Junior, whom we nicknamed "Chip" arrived July 20, 1949, robust and healthy except for some allergies he inherited from his father. We were ecstatic. He was everything we had hoped for.

I loved having a baby.

It was fun taking Chip for walks around the lovely little town and while pushing his baby carriage, I made the acquaintance of other young mothers also perambulating their little bundles from heaven. From those chance meetings there developed some of my closest friendships.

We had so much in common and lots to talk about, sharing with elation the joys of motherhood, and struggling together with the trials and tribulations of our new responsibilities. We all worked on our yards, took care of our children and houses, and enjoyed the company and love of our husbands when they returned from earning the family living.

He Gives Us Hope

For diversity I joined a bridge club, played a little tennis, and participated in the local little theater group.

Shark and I played bridge in a duplicate bridge club for a while (I was not very good but he was a whiz). We had a number of good friends among our peers, plus a lovely couple who were our near neighbors who acted like grandparents to Chip.

Business was good and Shark was a marvelous salesman and loved his work. One day he came home with a real surprise for me, a car of my own, which was not only a luxury but really a necessity since he was gone from home usually Monday through Friday, four weeks out of six.

Then an opportunity arose for us to buy a twin engine pleasure boat which greatly enhanced our times for recreation. After enjoying lovely days on Norris Lake, and evenings came, Chip loved being lulled to sleep by the rocking of the waves as he lay in the tiny cabin below.

After Chip was a year old we wanted to have another baby wishing that the children could be about two years apart. That fact was not to be accomplished quite on our time schedule as we had hoped, but finally we were blessed with a beautiful little baby girl on October 4, 1951. Lucette Ernestine Sharkey came to further grace our lives. She was a joy, and Chip loved having his baby sister.

Time marched on and we continued in the pattern that was established in our lives until, on June 12, 1953, we were again smiled on by Almighty God by being given the gift of another son. Conrad Griffith Sharkey, whom we called "Griff," joined the happy family. He was a love and lots of fun. Shark and I were by then in our early thirties.

I certainly had what most people would guess to be a fulfilling life with three lovely children, a wonderful husband who had a good job, a car of my own, household help twice a week, social acceptance, a nice house, a boat, in fact most of the material things I desired. We were not wealthy by any means but we lived very comfortably.

I was enamored of pretty clothes and proud of the fact that I was able to buy some of the name brands. A friend of mine who was a designer and creator of ladies' hats made mine for me, explicitly, at a rather exorbitant price. My makeup was especially chosen for my particular skin tones and I wore much more than I now consider to be becoming.

I played bridge about once a week and we drank quite a bit socially. I am grateful to say that I never drank by myself, nor did Shark when he was on the road. He had been warned against that by a fellow salesman. His evenings were usually spent calling on customers, small "truck jobbers" who operated out of their homes, or doing paper work in his hotel room.

Unfortunately, I had a bad habit of telling off-color jokes. I really felt that it was the "cute" thing to do, that I was a very chic modern woman.

I guess I was trying to live up to some sort of an image that I, or the commercialized world with its secular emphasis had created, the sophisticated suburban housewife.

I was resentful of my husband's being gone a lot in his lucrative job as a manufacturer's representative.

I realize in retrospect that his being away provided me with valuable time to pursue a number of activities and hobbies which have added much fulfillment to my life. Had he been around all the time I wonder if I would have attempted them.

At the time I certainly was not aware of the positive aspect of the circumstances. I felt very sorry for myself. I was quite self-centered.

We did not attend any church. We were not consciously avoiding God, we just were not paying any attention to Him. Nor were we mad at God. We just felt that we did not need Him. In fact, we most likely did not think of Him much, if at all. Why bother to go to church? Let God go His way and we would go ours.

Our manner of thinking was that we felt that we deserved the time relaxing together on the weekends on our boat and sleeping in on Sunday mornings because Shark worked hard and we needed that time together alone.

In the midst of it all I was instinctly aware that something was missing.

I am sure that my friends, at least my Christian friends, could see that I was spiritually needy. I feel sure that they prayed for me and for that I am eternally grateful.

My husband and I had both been brought up in Christian homes. We had attended Sunday School and church regularly as children. For that and the love and prayers of our parents we are very thankful.

Christian upbringing at the time in our lives when we are young and unable to discern for ourselves is tremendously important. It implants good values into one's subconscious mind. Those values become a part of one's being.

God has given us the precious freedom of choice which He has never taken away.

I think that if the seeds of Christian nurture have been sown, an individual who begins to explore the highways and byways and tries to find his way outside the Christian community will very likely "come to his senses" at some point in time.

It does not upset me that a young adult stays away from church for a while. I feel that when he or she reaches some stage in life (and it seems to happen at varying ages) the void will eventually send him searching.

Certainly one of the underlying reasons for experimentation in drugs, alcohol, sex, astrology, the occult, etc., is the search for meaning and answers to our lives.

Our seeking, desiring, longing is for God. There is a God-made place in each of us that only God our Creator can fill.

To quote St. Augustine of Hippo, "God made man for Himself and our hearts are restless until they rest in Him."

Jesus Christ is the way, the truth, and the life. Each individual has to find and accept Him personally as his Lord and Savior. No one can do it for him. The story of the prodigal son is a timeless one.

As for the persons who never have been exposed to Christian nurture, God is always there and waiting, and ready to respond to them when they ask.

As a result of our longing we began seeking, in the right direction. It was a beginning.

We began to turn to God.

Although we did not think that we needed church ourselves, we felt that our four-year-old son, Chip, did and so we took him to Sunday School. We deposited him, yelling and screaming quite often, and picked him up when it was over. The Sunday School teachers assured us that he would be all right and soon stop crying, which he always seemed to do, and we kept bringing him back and picking him up. "A little child shall lead them."

In time we decided to attend church ourselves, the people were so nice and one does feel a sense of guilt in doing what we were doing, leaving our son and depositing him week after week.

The church where we made this venture was St. Francis Episcopal Church in Norris. The place and congregation will always be very dear to our hearts.

It was a small congregation with very warm loving people. A little church in particular needs every member and it was a good feeling to be wanted and needed. Shark and I have always desired to be in small churches.

I was asked to bring cookies for a number of occasions, food for covered dish suppers, and to be a part in setting up and cleaning up. Those times will remain in my memory as fun times as they are to many people. Much camaraderie and valuable sharing takes place during those encounters.

He Gives Us Hope

St. Francis people became our real friends. They brought soup to us when one of us was sick, or just to share, in Christian love. They loaned me a car if mine was out of commission. We received cakes and surprises for our birthdays. I was asked to drop by for a cup of coffee or tea and a visit with many of the parishioners and we were included in some activities involving their families.

Chip got so that he looked forward to going and had some pals in the Sunday School group. He really liked the teachers, too. Lucette and Griff were in the groups provided for their respective ages. We were finally there as a family, in the presence of a real church family.

The people of that church accepted me just the way I was and in no way intimated that I would be much more pleasant to be with, or any happier, if I were different.

The very special friends to me were the good listeners to whom I could unburden my cares. I was able to tell them candidly things that were bothering me, the way I felt deep down inside. They were friends I could trust and then leave, knowing full well that whatever I revealed would not be repeated.

Oh, how grateful I am for their understanding and example. I count them more precious than jewels.

I believe we can all become God's agents as instruments of His healing power. One of the ways is to become good listeners.

Our hurtful experiences tend to be like wounds which become infected when they are not attended to. The longer they stay inside us, the more they fester and hurt. Only when we go to someone to have them treated, do they begin to heal. If they are left unattended the poison from the wounds spreads to other parts of the body and makes us sick all over.

Jesus can use us as listeners. I think that was part of His intention for His body, the Church.

Think of yourself in the role of the listener. All you have to have are big ears, an understanding heart, and a closed mouth so not to divulge the confidences you hear.

No great capacity for problem solving is required, nor is advice often needed.

When a person comes to me and pours out of her heart the experience that is troubling her, I am enabling my friend to open the wound in her soul or spirit, so that the poison, the infection can be disposed of.

Any wound, after being cleansed, will usually heal by itself, but if salve or ointment of some sort is applied at the time of cleansing, the wound will not only heal more quickly but it is less likely that the infection will return.

The salve or ointment, so to speak, with which I cover the wound is love, God's love. Love has great healing power and since God is Love, God heals my friend.

There are times when a friend's experience touches a familiar note in my own life. When that happens, I recall how God helped me in my dilemma, and often I relate to my friend the steps that might be of help to her, as they were to me. I feel that I would be remiss if I had a possible answer and kept it to myself.

When we pray as we listen and ask God for the guidance of the Holy Spirit, He will sometimes put thoughts in our minds or words in our mouths that will help in the healing process.

God knows the answers and we do not and it is God's desire to heal His people.

A large factor in the healing of relationships is the acceptance of people the way they are.

Jesus Christ was the only perfect person. It follows that no human being can be perfect. There will always be some imperfections. So there is no way we can will people or pray them into being the persons we would like for them to be.

We lift them up in prayer to God who knows their every need. He deals with them in those needs.

We know that God can change them as He sees fit, so that He can use them for His purposes (that is, if they, in their God-given freedom of choice respond).

We must let go and let God. He knows how much changing is possible, and when. Our timing is not His timing.

We must put the other person in God's hands and let Him do the transforming. He is their God, we are not. If we assume the role of being their God, we are out of step with Him and with them.

We wait for God to initiate the moves. We do not force situa-

20   He Gives Us Hope

tions. If we are used as instruments of God in the process, we are indeed grateful. We try to listen for His instructions and be obedient servants.

Healing is usually a gradual process. God knows all the factors involved. Some of these factors may be other relationships that must be dealt with before another step can take place. We cannot know all of these because we are not God.

We must accept the fact that the person may not change.

We do know that we can trust God implicitly.

Chip, Griff and Lucette

Chapter 3
I CAN HARDLY BELIEVE IT

The direction of one's life is often fascinating. People, places, experiences all go together to constitute the warp and woof of the fabric of life just as surely as varying colors of threads make up the fabric of woven cloth.

As I look back I am rather glad that I had my particular background of experience, because in our life in the ministry I can readily relate to the sophisticated bored suburban housewife, since I had known that role. Furthermore, if we had not had the opportunity of acquiring more than adequate material possessions, I might never have realized that they were not the answer to happiness in my life. Having grown up in the midst of depression years I had not known such "gracious plenty" and I had the feeling that if I could only reach those "heights" I would be blissfully content. One can gain deep insight by seeing things in retrospect.

In relating to wives with similar sets of circumstances (and I find many who fit into that category) I am grateful that I feel no disdain for them, only understanding and hope. My deep joy is in being able to picture them with fulfilled lives and radiantly happy faces. It is very exciting to see that possibility and have a desire to help in some way.

The best way I know of helping is in much the same manner as our friends helped me, by praying for me and being nice.

We were not Episcopalians. We had both been brought up as Presbyterians, but since there was no Presbyterian church in Norris, we had discovered St. Francis.

Shark and I both had a slight familiarity with the Episcopal church from attending the Christmas Eve midnight services in our respective home towns when we were growing up. We were each drawn to that service yearly although we did not understand the Eucharist. In our first year of marriage, while Shark was on Navy duty at the Sub Chaser Training School in Miami, Florida, we had attended our first Episcopal service together on Christmas Eve in that city.

He Gives Us Hope

St. Francis Church in Norris was a mission, not yet self-supporting. The congregation was small. Most of the members looked happy and seemed to really enjoy church, its worship, and their fellowship together. They possessed a very special quality which we unconsciously desired.

I remember watching one lady on her knees Sunday after Sunday prior to the service. She was obviously in prayerful conversation with "someone." Her quiet reverence and that of other members of the flock was appealing as they anticipated the beginning of the worship service.

After taking our children for a while and then going ourselves, occasionally, we began to attend on a regular basis. When we became progressively more active we eventually took the necessary and informative instructions from the priest and were confirmed as Episcopalians.

We had new friends, new interests, and it was fun, but confirmation is a beginning and not an end.

Some of my beliefs were not very clear to me. As had happened in my previous religious training, I was learning about God and Jesus, but had yet to have an experience that I could identify as that of knowing Jesus in person, and I did not know whether or not I knew God. Neither did I have a very realistic conception of the Holy Spirit. The third person of the Trinity was only a name to me, and it seems that when I was a child He was referred to more often as the Holy Ghost, which name made Him even more nebulous.

One day when our priest came to call, I asked him how I should know if I knew God.

Often Hank would not give a direct answer but would instead tell us to read a particular passage of scripture, as he did with me in that particular instance.

The scripture was from First John, chapter 4, verses 7 and 8.

When he left I found my Bible and read, "Beloved, let us love one another: for love is of God; and everyone that loveth is born of God, and knoweth God. He that loveth not knoweth not God; for God is love" (KJV).

I thought to myself, I know what love is. I love my husband, my children, my parents, my sisters, my friends. Wow! I know

God! The simplicity and impact of that reality staggered me.

Had I been trying to confound a beautifully simple thought into some great theological concept so complicated as to elude my mind?

Had I not been able to see the forest for the trees? Do we try to complicate other things that should be simple?

Jesus said, "Verily I say unto you, Except ye be converted and become as little children, ye shall not enter into the kingdom of heaven" (Matthew 18:3, KJV).

I began to believe and trust in that simple and childlike way.

Another episode that stands out in my memory as clearly as if it were yesterday, had my kitchen as its setting. I was standing by myself asking the question, "What in the hell is life all about?" Yes, I swore a bit in those days, too.

I suddenly saw my life in capsule form in my mind, the life I knew. It consisted of getting up in the morning, washing, ironing, cleaning, the never-ending housewife syndrome. I saw myself as a child, growing up, getting married, having children, then envisioned their marrying, our having grandchildren, then members of the family dying off. It all seemed so incomplete. I felt "there must be more to life than this."

Then it began to happen.

As Jesus said in His sermon on the mount: "Ask, and it shall be given you; seek, and ye shall find; knock and it shall be opened unto you: For everyone that asketh receiveth; and he that seeketh findeth; and to him that knocketh it shall be opened" (Matthew 7: 8, KJV).

Our Lord is just waiting for us to want, need, to feel an emptiness. Then He can enter our lives and fill them with Himself, and we really begin to live.

I began to ask, I began to seek, I opened the door a crack and the Lord came in. Very gradually, but unmistakably He changed my life. I had a real conversion.

Conversion means to turn around in a different direction and that is exactly what I did. My sense of values changed, my attitudes toward family and friends all changed, and I began to see everything in a new light. It was fascinating.

I remember sneaking off one afternoon by myself to a little town about six miles away to see a movie put out by a Christian film company and featuring a Christian family and their life. It was beautiful. I sneaked deliberately because of fear of rejection and ridicule that I felt I might get from some of my sophisticated and secularly oriented friends.

Recalling the words of the familiar Christmas hymn, "Oh, Little Town of Bethlehem," think of the verse that says, "How silently, how silently, the wondrous gift is given! So God imparts to human hearts the blessings of His heaven. No ear may hear His coming, yet in this world of sin, where meek souls will receive Him, still, the dear Christ enters in."

He does enter our lives and live in us. Our lives do change!

The heavy makeup began to disappear. I stopped swearing and telling the dirty jokes because I found that our Lord shows us a much more beautiful way and good things come out of our mouths because He puts good thoughts and feelings in our hearts and minds.

It no longer seemed necessary or even fun to drink a lot. You do not have to wonder the next day what you said the night before when you had too much to drink. You surely felt better in the morning when you had to get up early and feed the children.

He affected my life in every way. I began to look forward to different things and to spend my time to better advantage, not so much for myself as I had before, but for others.

Please do not misunderstand me, one does not suddenly become completely unselfish, but Jesus changes the parts of our lives that we let Him.

There was such a complete change in me that about ten years later, when I was attending a conference at our diocesan center, I came upon a lady from Norris with whom I had played bridge years before and the lady said to me, "You are Connie Sharkey, are you not?"

I answered, "Yes."

She said, "You look like a completely different person!"

I replied, "I am, by the grace of God."

I was so excited that I could have jumped on the closest rooftop and shouted with joy. I knew that there had been a change in me because I could feel it, but for someone else to visibly see it was the most thrilling thing that I could imagine. You can see the Lord in other people.

He lives as the Creator of the universe who never stops creating. He lives as the resurrected Lord. He lives in people who believe that Jesus Christ is the Son of God.

"Now ye are the body of Christ, and members in particular" (I Corinthians 12:27, KJV). That is what the church is called, the body of Christ. The church is the body, of which Christ is the head.

Shark became involved in the activities of the church in a variety of capacities. The men of St. Francis were actually building their house of worship with their own hands, an exciting labor of love, and Shark began helping them. He loved doing it and was there on the scene more and more.

Since his job also took him away it bothered me that he was spending more time away from home, but somehow since this was at the church, I felt that it was good. Nevertheless it still exasperated me and I felt guilty.

I did not know how to handle my feelings about the situation so I made an appointment with our priest to talk it over. In our conversation I identified the culprit, since I knew it was jealousy, and told the priest in an informal, but real confession. He listened and we prayed about it. The outcome was that either by his suggestion or on my own initiative, I decided to go up to the church and help, too. I pounded nails and had a ball. It was really fun and completely eradicated the jealousy.

I think that God allows problem areas to surface so that we can see our weaknesses. He could take care of them, but then how would we grow? We aren't puppets, we are human beings with consciences and wills.

When we are faced with temptations, we can readily see those that present no problems to us whatsoever (the ones we can easily overcome) and by the same token we have our eyes opened wide (sometimes with shock and pain to our prides and egos) to discover our Achilles heel.

He Gives Us Hope

In school a test enables both teacher and pupil to discern what the student already knows and where he is weak and therefore needs further instruction, discipline, as well as support. Quite often he is tested again in the same subject matter to ascertain his development.

I believe life is like that. We grow in grace as we are strengthened by the Holy Spirit. He teaches us His way.

St. Paul said that when he was weak he was strong because he had to depend on the Lord, and the Lord always came through with the help he needed. In His might we are strengthened and we go "on our way rejoicing" (Hymn 568, Episcopal Hymnal).

I was aware that Shark was becoming more and more interested in the church. He was, in fact, gradually spending more time in activities connected with St. Francis and becoming less desirous of going out on the road.

In the course of time he made arrangements for personal study under the tutelage of our dear friend, the Reverend Doctor William Pollard.

Bill, who had entered the priesthood, was a renowned physicist, and together with his job with the Atomic Energy Commission, had been interim priest-in-charge of St. Francis before they had a full-time priest. He, having studied outside of seminary, was in an excellent position to guide Shark toward what he hoped would be the perpetual diaconate.

As a perpetual deacon, Shark would continue his vocation as a salesman but become ordained in the church to assist the priest in whatever capacity the priest required of him.

Frankly, I was not sold on that idea as I knew that when Shark attempted a project he threw himself into it completely, and I did not see how he could do justice to either or both jobs. I felt also that there might not be any time left for the family, including me.

At that point I said nothing about my feelings and he continued to pursue his studies as well as his job as a salesman.

In the meantime he and others were praying for both of us.

A while later, and how long a time span had elapsed I cannot remember, but I do recall that the occasion occurred during Holy week (the time of our Lord's passion) while we were having a most interesting conversation, one in fact that ultimately changed the course of our lives.

I posed the question to Shark, "You want to go into the priesthood, don't you?" The priesthood is a step beyond the diaconate and usually requires seminary. As a priest the person most often follows that as his full-time vocation.

He looked at me with surprise and amazement and replied, "Yes, how did you know that?"

My answer was, "I don't know how, I just know." I understand now that the Holy Spirit told me, but I did not realize that at the time. It made no difference that I could not identify the source, I just knew it was so.

Shark asked me next, "How do you feel about it?," and I said that I thought it would be great and "let's go!"

He told me that he wanted to become a priest but that he did not feel that he could take me out of the kind of life we were living, knowing full well that we would make much less money, and so would not be able to afford many of the things we had grown accustomed to having. He had been treasurer of St. Francis and so knew how little some priests make.

That made no difference to me, I was excited and I really wanted him to pursue his dream. Actually he did not "dream it up." He had in fact been driving down a road in Tennessee in the course of his travels, in his job, and the Lord had spoken to him and said, "I want you to be one of my priests." My husband was so startled he almost ran off the road. He pulled over to the shoulder, stopped the car and sat there and just shook. After gaining his composure, he resumed his drive. Still to this day he can take anyone to that spot where it happened. One day on a trip we went by there.

After discussing it together in much more depth he went to our priest, Hank Myers, to tell him and ask his advice about it.

Instead of Hank's being surprised and seemingly pleased, Shark said he had a "different" look on his face which puzzled Shark and which he interpreted as displeasure, or something like that.

Shark said, "What's the matter, don't you think I would be a good priest?" whereupon Hank replied, "Yes, I think you'd be a very good one, but I have one question for you. What took you so long? I've known it for a good while!"

The Lord had spoken to all three of us. There was no doubt in our minds that the Lord wanted Shark to be a priest.

The next step was to follow the necessary procedures in church red tape for admittance to seminary. Being recommended by the priest and council of one's church is among the first. Then one must be approved by the bishop of the diocese and the church's "standing committee," a diocesan body.

The candidate is also required to have a complete psychiatric and physical examination. Those precautionary measure help cull out the misfits.

It is a lot to go through and a person must be very serious about his vocation to be a priest to complete all the necessary requirements and qualifications, plus he must have a college degree in most cases. Shark had satisfied that necessity when we had gone back to Chapel Hill after World War II. We realized that the Lord had been in the midst of that decision, too, and had undoubtedly been preparing us for a long time.

We took one step at a time, praying all the while, and finally our anticipation was relieved when we found out that Shark had been accepted.

We were excited and a little scared but we knew that the Lord was with us and would help us all the way.

It was a long time before we finally went to seminary as there were many more preparations to be taken care of and much more water to go over the dam in our lives as individuals and as a family.

Shark and Connie

Chapter 4
"OFFER IT"

Have you ever gone through a valley of real physical pain? Pain that made tears run down your cheeks as you talked to a friend in a grocery store parking lot, involuntary tears that you couldn't control? I have, and it is a helpless feeling.

My thirtieth birthday had rolled around, and this is a flashback before our decision to go to seminary. It was a very important one in my training and thinking and so I share it with you with gratitude.

The birthday wasn't the problem–it was my back. Because of it my thirtieth birthday was actually the most difficult I have faced, each decade since then has really posed no particular problem.

In picking up our darling chubby daughter out of the back of the station wagon, I had lifted her incorrectly (there is a proper way to lift I have since found out) and I did something.

I tried rest, a chiropractor, our family doctor, and finally at the latter's suggestion went to an orthopedic surgeon who found out that I was born with one too many vertebrae, the extra one being incomplete, and in a critical spot in the curve of my spine. I had been lucky for thirty years that it had caused me no trouble but now it had popped out of place and was excruciating, pressing on nerves so that pain went up to my neck and down my leg. It hurt nearly all the time.

The orthopedic surgeon taught me a good lesson. As I lay on his examining table he asked if I had anything bothering me. I did not answer affirmatively. He asked a second time and I gave him no real answer. Then he left the room, somewhat exasperated.

When he went out I thought to myself, "You dummy, he's trying to help you, tell him. You went to a doctor to find out what is wrong, talk to him!"

So I asked him to come back and said, "Yes, I have something bothering me." I related that my husband was gone from home a lot because of his job, and often I had the full responsibility of the children, and now I had just been elected president of our women's group at church. (They had seen that I was interested and eager and had thought they had given me something special.) I was so new in the church that I didn't even know what it was all about, and I am not very good at telling people what to do or delegating responsibility.

That kind, understanding and perceptive doctor told me that he was giving me doctor's orders to give up the presidency. The children were my first and natural responsibility and I loved taking care of them so I should continue to do that, but he felt I was carrying too heavy a load with the other added on and I must let it go.

I was absolutely elated! Gloriously relieved! I didn't know I could feel so much better. That was the beginning.

I was also fitted for a steel and leather back brace which at first I shunned wearing, and later welcomed, and wore for a year with deep gratitude. It held the vertebrae in place until healing took place and with daily exercises I was able to strengthen the muscles to eventually do without the brace. To this day I know my limitations with lifting and pulling at certain angles. There are some things I simply cannot do because of the congenital condition, for which surgery was not deemed wise, or even suggested, and I accepted the fact. All these years later I have the same back and have learned to live with it comfortably.

The doctor also suggested that I hire full-time help, someone to live in, and he forbade me to pick up my baby Lucette. That crushed me and I felt very guilty for not doing so, but that was the way it had to be.

Luckily we were able to afford having a woman come into our home and we were able to find someone. I am grateful to Almighty God for His providence.

The long period of recuperation when I was unable to do much physically was very frustrating to me.

One day of that time span our priest came to see me. When I told Hank how ill-at-ease I was he said, "Offer it." I asked what he meant and in his inimitable style, which sometimes infuriated me, he gave no explanation but repeated, "Offer it."

I hadn't a clue to what I was doing but, as I have mentioned before, I had begun to acquire a childlike faith and acceptance and decided to do just that, "offer it." I figured God would know what

Hank was talking about even if I didn't, and so I acquiesced and offered it to God. What I presume was offered was the whole package about my back and all it entailed.

I had no idea what would happen, and I am not able to exactly put my finger on what did, but something very beautiful and profound took place. God used that entire experience in most unique ways.

For the most part, He seemed to use me to help others who were going through similar painful situations. It was absolutely remarkable. Many other individuals benefited by my suffering just because the Lord God knows how to turn problem situations into victories.

Not only were my friends the recipients of His grace, part of my life was transformed. He taught me new compassion for my fellow man and began to turn my thoughts away from myself to the direction and needs of others.

A new door had been opened for me. It was exciting. God's power is unbelievable. God gives us the victory.

As He transformed the death of His Son, an awful thing, into the glory of His resurrection, so He is able to transform our trials into resurrection experiences.

Ever since that time, whenever I have an unpleasantness (and life is full of them), I offer it to God knowing that He will use it to His glory.

In time I have had sense enough to offer not only the bad but the good to Him. After all, why should we come to Him only with our problems? He certainly desires to use our joys as well. Later I want to give ample time and space to what happens when we begin to give thanks.

I have witnessed beautiful things in the lives of many others who have turned to the Lord in their times of trial. My sisters, for example. When Peg was in her early thirties she had to be hospitalized for almost a year, with tuberculosis, which meant that she was away from her three little girls and her husband. She recovered fully and was so very grateful. One kidney had to be removed in the process. During her extended confinement she naturally experienced despair, loneliness, frustration, and all the feelings that

He Gives Us Hope

accompany a long illness.

She told me after she had come out of the hospital that some day, in some way, she was going to help people who had to be confined to a hospital away from their families. She did not know where it would be.

Although her college degree was in another field and she had no academic training for her job, she was radiantly happy as

Peg and Bob Dalton

an activity therapist at a mental hospital in Cincinnati. Her real forte was her loving compassion and understanding with the patients, who were her friends. She planned outings to the ball park, trips to the zoo, birthday parties, church services, square dances, you name it, she did it, and they loved it and her.

I have visited the hospital with her and seen the patients look at her with loving eyes and big smiles. She did more than many people who have the formal training and not much heart. Hers was a real vocation. Her love came through and the patients responded. Peg knew how to encourage them and to help them find self-worth, plus having fun.

Her aim was to make them enjoy as best they could their confinement, as long as they had to be there, and to help them learn to adjust for the outside world when possible and to be happy useful human beings.

She started out as a volunteer, part-time, and was later a paid staff member in charge of her department. Alive, vibrant, fun, attractive, much younger looking than many people her age, with her husband pursuing his own vocation and their three lovely girls grown and living elsewhere in the country, Peg told me concerning her chosen work, "Con, every day I look forward to going, I just love my work." She had a well-founded life which included family, church, tennis, entertaining in her home, as well as visiting with close friends, and real fulfillment in her life. I am certainly proud that she is my sister. She went to her reward in 1989 at the age of 69.

I am equally proud of my older sister, Fran, who has been an inspiration. While she and Jerry, who has always been a Roman Catholic, were dating, Fran became very interested in his church, took instruction, and was confirmed.

Her faith sustained her through many trials and tribulations.

Fran and Jerry both worked at the same place and were joyfully married in 1941 full of hope for the future. Then Jerry was one of the first group of young men to be drafted. He was in the thick of World War II in the Pacific.

While Jerry was overseas, Fran and her little girl, Nancy, came back home to live with Mother and Daddy and me, while continuing her job as a

Jerry & Fran Tiettmeyer

receptionist at a Coca Cola plant. I can remember her anxiety and how she dealt with it while Jerry was out of the country.

The Catholic church was right up the street from where we lived and every day Fran went to church.

The terrible news that her loving husband was wounded in battle and had to have one of his legs amputated came with its attendant shock.

Fran continued stopping in at the church every day.

When Jerry was brought back to this country and entered a hospital in Texas for further surgery, Fran joined him. It was because she was with Jerry that Fran was unable to attend Shark's and my wedding in Chapel Hill. We were certainly together in spirit.

The struggle that ensued for the two of them and their darling daughter and baby boy was a rough one, which they faced valiantly. Jerry and Fran eventually got an apartment, and with the help of

He Gives Us Hope

the Lord, their church, and their families and friends, they pulled their lives together. With Jerry's rehabilitation, he entered a different kind of work where he could sit and not have to be on his feet all the time.

I marveled at how they handled the situation, how Fran sustained Jerry without babying him, and how my brother-in-law's Christian faith and strength along with his wonderful sense of humor were so healing to everyone.

Cincinnati was way too hot and humid in the summer and the snow and ice were treacherous in the winter, so in time, trained for a new job in computers, Jerry moved with his little family of four to California which is more temperate.

They were still there and continued to be beautiful servants for the Lord. They both use to play golf and he worked with handicapped children. Fran had her church friends and prayer group, and their children and grandchildren were nearby. Jerry died at the age of 79 and Fran at 82.

God does take care of us and our needs when we trust Him and He can turn any situation that is offered to Him into triumph.

Offer it.

Chapter 5
CONSIDER THE LILIES OF THE FIELD

In the early stages of my searchings the Lord taught me one of the most beautiful lessons I have learned, and one which I continue to use to this day.

In our service of Holy Communion there are what are called the "comfortable words." They are from the sayings of Jesus, and the following are His words: "Come unto me all ye that travail and are heavy laden, and I will refresh you" (Book of Common Prayer, p. 332).

That sentence really popped out at me one day in church. I decided to take it literally, to really believe what He said. As a result, every time I felt bad or tired or low I would think of Jesus and say those words. I found out that He really did mean them. He helped me every time.

The help at times came in the form of a friend's unexpected phone call, or letter, or even a visit. At other times it was a sudden feeling to stop work and fix myself a cup of tea, or possibly take a walk, where I would once again become aware of the beauties of nature in the world. This awareness came only after I had acted on the suggestion He brought to my mind. Often one has to take action before a change will occur. As I walked I saw lovely trees and shrubs in all their strength and beauty, breathtaking cloud formations, heard the songs of birds, and in the spring saw the first jonquils heralding new life and giving us renewed hope.

The phone calls, letters, and visits would show me that I was not alone and that someone was thinking of me and caring enough to take the time to call, write, or come by.

There were even instances when I would perhaps had been feeling sort of sorry for myself, and after I had said that prayer or turned to the Lord (which is really what I was doing), He would lead me in thought or in person to a place which made me realize how well off I was, such as to the bedside of an ill friend. In a hospital or sickroom I do not think the average person feels self-pity after seeing those who are incapacitated or hurting.

36   He Gives Us Hope

Reading a book could show me how very rich in relationships and love I was. It never failed. Every single time I asked, He helped me, and seldom in the same way, but always in the manner that would best alleviate my condition at that particular moment of my life.

What a beautiful lesson: He was teaching me to trust Him, that He absolutely meant every word He said.

Going to seminary was to be an exciting step for us and an awesome change in our lifestyle in many ways.

We knew that seminary would be expensive and that Shark would no longer have the income from his job, so we began trying to save money in every conceivable way. Putting what we could in savings was the first step but somehow we were not very successful. Then we sold my car to add to our savings account, which step also avoided the gas and insurance expenses plus future repair bills. That was right before I went to the hospital to deliver Hilary, our new little bundle from heaven.

Hilary Faye Sharkey was born in January 31, 1957, another beautiful baby girl. She was a joy and still is.

Strangely enough that act of selling my car put me in the position of having to learn to receive, more than ever before in my life. I had enjoyed giving. Receiving graciously is a gift, I believe.

Shark was still traveling and naturally with four small children, three of whom were not yet in school but at home with me, I had unexpected trips to the doctor or grocery store in addition to regularly scheduled ones, and at times I just had the desire to get out of the house.

I could not rely on someone giving me a casual call or dropping by. Instead of passively waiting, I had to actively make requests stating my needs, which is often humbling.

People were lovely to me. I found out, too, which of our friends sincerely meant it when they asked me to call on them when I had a need. Those were very special people who would do anything they could to help in a pinch, often requiring considerable rearrangements of their own responsibilities. Their examples inspired me to do likewise for others.

It was a joy being part of that love relationship between good friends. God was acting.

We planned to go to seminary when we could afford it. Our house went up for sale and there were no prospective buyers. Our bank account increased slowly as month after month went by, and we realized that we would not in any foreseeable future be able to save the money necessary to sustain our family during the coming seminary experience.

After several months and very much soul-searching and prayer, we finally decided that if God really wanted us in the ministry, he would help us get through when we worked as hard as we could, and trusted Him. So we took a "leap of faith" and decided to go!

When Shark went to Sewanee to have the interview with the dean of the seminary, our plan that Shark be there for only two years was altered by the dean and our bishop, who both wanted him there for the full three years and not as a "special student." Money had been our only drawback, so being advised to take the extra year, and really ready to proceed, we were again willing to trust God and go for three.

The bishop of our diocese could help us out to a small degree financially, $500.00 a year, but that was all. The church at Oak Ridge, Tennessee, offered Shark their scholarship fund for his tuition and Shark planned to get a part-time job on campus while he was going to school.

As I have expressed before, we were blessed with some very wonderful and faithful friends with whom we had been growing in the church. I feel sure you will agree with me when I tell you the extent of their loyalty and unselfishness.

The men in two of the families, in addition to their vocations, dabbled in real estate. To our absolute joy and wonder, Harry Reynolds and Frank Manning bought our house from us for the asking price, knowing full well that they might not in turn be able to sell it any time soon since it had already been on the market.

We loved our home, our first, and had worked very hard toward getting it fixed up the way we wanted it, doing much of the remodeling work ourselves. Now we were leaving it.

We had toyed with the idea of renting it in the event we were unable to sell it, but we would have been burdened with the huge

38   He Gives Us Hope

responsibility of upkeep from considerable distance.

The generous act of our friends not only enriched our bank account, it fed our hearts and souls, and got the monkey off of our backs of the responsibility of renting. We were filled with deep gratitude. Theirs was an act of pure Christian stewardship and charity.

Charity was not the only reaction expressed by our friends and acquaintances concerning our decision to enter seminary. Some thought we were out of our minds, downright crazy to be leaving "security" to be followers of Jesus and going into the life of His ministry.

Shark had some very interesting conversations with his customers on his last round of his territory as a salesman when he told them why he was leaving. A number of them expressed their religious feelings to him for the first time. He felt this to be the beginning of his ministry.

In August of 1957 we moved to Sewanee, Tennessee, for Shark to enter the School of Theology of the University of the South, known to most people as "St. Luke's" (St. Luke's being the name of the hall in which the seminary was then housed).

Chip, our oldest son, was eight years old, Lucette was six, Griff was four, and Hilary, our youngest daughter, just nine months.

The process of moving was in itself startling because of the fact that the driver underestimated the contents of the house and did not bring a large enough van. In our effort to save money we had engaged a man who was "moonlighting" in that business and was inexperienced.

At midnight on a warm summer night we found ourselves sitting in the front yard on covered mattresses, with our four children and our Schnauzer, Pepper, surrounded by an assortment of furniture and boxes, expectantly awaiting the return of the van for the second load.

The unusual spectacle was illuminated by a magnificent full moon. Thank goodness the weather was warm and dry and we were eager to embark on our new adventure.

Ultimately the van arrived, was loaded with the rest of our belongings, and we piled the whole family and the dog into the car and took off.

Arriving in Sewanee at approximately daybreak we headed straight for "Bairnwick," the spacious and fascinating home of the parents of our priest and friend, Hank Myers. His father, Dr. George Myers, was then on the faculty of the seminary.

Bless their hearts, they acted like it was nothing out of the ordinary. Mrs. Myers, having been aroused from sleep, welcomed us with open arms, fixed a nice hot breakfast for all of us and then prepared beds for the children who went out like lights.

George and Margaret Myers had raised, in that unique home, eight children, all of whom had grown and left the nest, so there was ample space to temporarily house our bedraggled and exhausted family. The extraordinary couple literally and figuratively took us under their wings, being to us like another set of parents.

We loved them both very much and "Mita," as Margaret Myers was affectionately known to some of us, became my spiritual mentor and dear friend.

Mita was quite a person. Among her many talents she had run her own school at Bairnwick, hiring a number of additional teachers, in order to give quality education to her children and some others in the community who wished to attend. She wrote religious drama and had been on the board of national church organizations along with being very active in community affairs. She held classes for the seminary wives in the instruction and proper care of the altar. A breath of fresh air for the seminarians and the wives of those who were married were the monthly teas at Bairnwick, hosted by Mita, giving all of us a delightful change of pace. She asked the wives to take turns helping her with the serving and pouring tea and cookies.

We moved into the upstairs of a house which had been given to the Diocese of Tennessee. It had formerly been the carriage house of a bishop long years ago and had been known as the Gailor Cottage. It had been partially renovated and occasionally used as a getaway place for clergy in the diocese, then given to be used as a home for two seminary families from Tennessee. Lee and George Kuhnert moved into the downstairs. A lot of money had been put into getting it ready for us but it was far from being completely

He Gives Us Hope

comfortable. It was a roof over our heads and it was rent free.

The "Tennessee House" as the cottage was newly christened was built on a hillside, putting the Kuhnerts at ground level also.

We Sharkeys had the main floor and an attic-type room above that which had no screens in the windows and no covering of any sort for the fiberglass insulation tacked up between the rafters.

When the children began itching, we realized that tiny particles of insulation were falling on their beds in one of the upstairs rooms we had set up dormitory style. Providing screens for the windows and putting up 4' x 8' sheets of plywood to cover the insulation became our number one priority for the house.

Before we had put the screens in, a humorous incident occurred. One night a little bird flew in, awakened the children, and soon the whole family was engaged in a flutter of activity trying to direct the panicky little creature to an open window. Shark looked ever so much like a toreador as he lurched around the room waving a bright towel. The children thought it was hilarious. Somehow we were able to get the little bird outside safely and unhurt. We all laughed uproariously and eventually went back to bed. Our family had a lot of fun laughing together! The kids were so good about our change.

Shark at age 36 had been out of college and away from academic life for ten years. That proved to be a very difficult adjustment as seminary courses are hard, and of course on the graduate level.

He worked as student manager of St. Luke's bookstore, took a full schedule and studied at night into the wee small hours. Later, instead of the job at the bookstore he became secretary to the chaplain of the university, who was at that time David Collins.

David had mostly student wives as his secretaries and he was constantly losing them when their husbands graduated or oftentimes when they had babies. We all laughed with him in regard to his observation that he finally had one who wouldn't get pregnant. Shark was his first male secretary and they got along famously.

During our three years in Sewanee our children had a lot of sickness in addition to the usual childhood diseases. Some of their illnesses were due to the fact that the house was not at all well insulated. In fact, there were places where you could see light through cracks in the outside walls.

Despite the thousands of dollars that had been spent in renovation, much had been necessarily spent on new wiring and plumbing, and proper insulation had been neglected. Even with many eighty dollar a month heating bills, which in those days were enormous, the house that was set down among lots of trees and shrubs was often cold and damp.

We ran out of money in two years, our money.

Then we learned faith!

Many were the times when we would be down to our last dollar and money would come from somewhere, almost miraculously. It was like manna from heaven, time after time.

Once it was in the form of an income tax rebate which we had momentarily forgotten was due us. Friends who cared sent us checks "out of the blue" just to show us they cared. Various churches in the diocese gave us gifts of money.

He Gives Us Hope

One priest friend of ours, who also had been married when he was in seminary occasionally sent Shark a check with the express purpose of taking me out to dinner for a special treat.

One Christmas which Shark and I thought would be very bleak for the children and us turned out to be absolutely beautiful.

We had called the older children in to inform them of our situation so that they would be forewarned and not expect much of anything. Our Christmases in Norris had been lavish with toys and goodies. Chip and Lucette took the news very well. We felt that Griff and Hilary were too young to understand or be burdened.

Then lo and behold on December the twenty-third, on the night before Christmas Eve, two cars pulled up in our driveway, the back seats full to overflowing.

There was a knock on the door, and upon answering it we were greeted by several radiantly happy Christians from St. Stephens, Oak Ridge, the church from whom we received the yearly scholarship fund. They had driven the distance of at least one hundred and twenty miles (there were no interstates then) especially to see us and bring us their good tidings of great joy.

They carried into the house out of the cold winter night bags after bags of groceries, staples, and canned food of all kinds. The gift givers were even thoughtful enough to include such items as asparagus and cashew nuts as well as the ordinary foods we needed, and topping it all off was a huge turkey with all its accompaniments.

Back they went to the cars, next laden down with beautifully wrapped Christmas gifts for the whole family. An additional trip produced armloads of used, but very good, clothes for the children.

They were gloriously happy and we were overwhelmed and grateful beyond words.

We chatted for a short while, had a cup of coffee together, then thanked them again and said goodbye with tears of joy and love, wishing them a very Merry Christmas and Godspeed as they returned to their homes, families, and church for the celebration of Jesus' birth.

The next day I just had to share my joy with someone and so called Mary Alexander on the phone. Mary, the wife of the dean of the seminary, had been lovely to us always, welcoming me graciously into her home whenever I walked in that direction with Hilary and stopped in for a short visit. She had also brought us ice cream after Chip had had his tonsillectomy. Mary had teas at her home for us, as did Mita.

I related the events of the previous night, telling her of their beautiful gifts and visitation from the people of St. Stephens, and said that not everyone was a lucky as we were since I knew of other seminary families who were also having financial struggles and did not have such thoughtful churches remembering them in such a tangible way.

Mary was delighted and shared my joy, telling me that she knew we were going to be given the gifts. What warmth and love.

The women of another church in Tennessee, St. John's, Knoxville, made a contribution to all the seminary wives and which was a boost to me personally.

They became aware that many of us could not buy new clothes and, being women, knew that getting a new dress occasionally perked up one's spirits. As a consequence they issued a plea and collected a considerable amount of really nice clothing that they no longer needed, and sent them via some of their group to St. Luke's.

It was really neat to be able to obtain free of charge a good looking smart, practically new dress for a special occasion.

Fay Myers had been a help to me in my anticipation and preparation for seminary. She had been at General Seminary with Hank and knew from experience.

When we were getting ready to leave Norris, I, being a newly zealous Christian and not having everything in perspective, planned to give away the lovely four skin Kolinsky scarf that Shark had given me one Christmas. I felt then (but certainly do not now) that it was ostentatious and represented the materialism I had been enjoying and was ready and willing to give up. The mink is a pretty one and in that era fur scarves were worn with suits a lot. Many of my friends had ones similar to mine.

Faye in her wisdom said, "Connie, there are going to be times when you are so tired and broke and sick of it all that it will do you worlds of good to get all dressed up fit to kill and go someplace."

She was absolutely right and I thought of her whenever Satan reared his ugly head and tried to make me miserable and feel sorry for myself, as if I were some sort of a martyr.

And so it happened, time after time. When we would get down just to the point of despair, some loving soul or group would think of us and send love, prayers, strength, money, or whatever seemed to be our express need at the moment.

Not all the help came form out of town, much was given right there by friends. Betty was one such friend.

From the time we had first arrived in Sewanee in a totally new environment I was often in a dither learning my way around and finding out about schools, teachers, doctors, and the best place to shop for groceries.

It is so helpful to have someone well oriented to an environment who is willing and able to give tips and clarifying information. It seemed that almost every time I was in that kind of a quandary, Betty would suddenly appear. Inevitably she would give me the information I needed. It was wonderful, like another gift from the Lord.

I feel sure that the Lord did bring us together because as we saw each other often and shared many thoughts and feelings we were able to help each other over some humps we were struggling with, in the realm of problems and hurts, that had not been dealt with.

I saw her freed of a burden she had carried for years (one she shared with me in confidence) and through prayers and her acceptance of God's grace and forgiveness she was like a butterfly out of its cocoon. The change was beautiful to behold and I was so happy for her.

She was a great help to me, too, especially one day, when she made a statement and asked me a question. She said, "Everyone else loves you, why don't you love yourself?" It made me think deeply.

The problem had to do with some of what I had been sharing with Betty. I was very resentful of my mother for something she had done years before and I felt guilty. (She had a problem with alcohol.)

I knew the Ten Commandments said to "Honor thy father and

thy mother" and I didn't feel that I was honoring my mother at all. The result was that I was carrying a heavy burden, guilt, and consequently did not like myself.

I was doing some reading of a spiritual nature since I was a probationer in the Society of the Companions of the Holy Cross, an international companionship of over 700 Episcopal women, living daily in the world under a rule of intercessory prayer, thanksgiving, simplicity of life, and special concern for unity, mission, and social justice. Faye and Mita had sponsored me while we were still in Norris.

Through reading the devotional material the subject of "listening prayer" was brought to my attention. It sounded fascinating.

I felt that I would dearly love to hear the Lord's voice and have Him speak to me, but I thought it was a possibility way beyond my capabilities. Still I wanted it to happen.

My reasoning was that if God loves us and wants us to love Him in return, and has ordained us to be His instruments on earth, He would certainly provide a way of communicating with us in order to let us know what He wants us to do for Him.

I found out that one must be quiet in order to hear Him speak and that it helps to have "open channels" to hear God's voice.

I was learning a lot about "cleansed channels."

The following is a quotation that made tremendous impact on me: "The biggest thing that any human being can do is to make of himself a cleansed channel through which the powers of the other world may flow." (From "An Introduction to the Inner Life" by the Rt. Rev. Lumsden Barkway, D.D.)

Of course we cannot cleanse ourselves, only God can do that, but we can want to be cleansed, and be willing to be introspective for the length of time necessary to find out what needs cleansing. Then we ask God to do it for us. The action requires our cooperation. It is not a passive response.

Compare a person to a plant. Each branch of a plant is nourished by means of little channels or veins through which flow the life-giving substances necessary for the development of the plant. If a branch is damaged there is not a free flow of nourishment. Plant diseases and insect pests can attack the tender shoots which

He Gives Us Hope

are developing and thus drain off the life-giving substances, or work in opposition to them.

Think of our spiritual health working in the same manner. Hatred, fear, and resentment stop up the channels which carry the flow of God's grace.

When we hate, are afraid, or resent someone, we are being attacked from within and without by foreign elements which God's nature of love has to fight. Our inner beings, or consciences, know that something is amiss and alert our minds and bodies to the presence of the enemy.

Much of our energy is spent in rationalization, in reliving old experiences. In the process, precious time and effort are lost that could otherwise be productive.

Oftentimes when we hate, are afraid, or resentful, we in turn get mad at ourselves for doing so, thus losing more constructive energy.

We wonder why we do not have a good feeling or one of peace. It may well be that we are going contrary to the goodness or the will of God. Our lifeblood is being sapped and we are devoid of strength.

"I am the vine, ye are the branches" (John 15:5).

That is what the Lord told us. He said that if we abide in Him we shall flourish and bear fruit. If we do not we shall wither and die.

Along with hatred, fear, and resentment are myriad other equally destructive emotions. Pride, envy, covetousness, jealousy, and self-centeredness (which is the root of all the rest) break down healthy relationships with God, our neighbors, and ourselves and walls or barriers arise. We become frustrated, feel isolated, unhappy, and everything seems to go wrong.

Negative emotions are distractions that keep us from going forward. Not until we recognize them as enemies, can we begin to fight them and get rid of the foes. We must acknowledge them to Almighty God and ask for forgiveness.

He is loving and desires to change them into positive emotions.

There are times that we need counseling. Other times outside help is not necessary, we can deal directly with our Creator.

God is His infinite mercy through Jesus' redemptive act, already accomplished for all mankind, hears us and lifts our guilt from us. Praise God.

When we accept His forgiveness we are again one with God and know the peace of God which passes all understanding. We are "ransomed, healed, restored, forgiven" as the beautiful hymn #282 expresses it. We become "cleansed channels" through which the love and power of God's world may flow.

God's love not only flows into us and gives us health of body and mind as well as spirit, that we need, but His love may then freely flow through us and out to others.

One aspect of being a cleansed channel that is so beautiful and exciting to me is that it does not matter who or where you are, what your vocation or station in life is, you can be a channel of God's grace.

I was able, through the knowledge that I had gained, to recognize my problem. I must say that I tried and tried to forgive my mother and was not able to do it easily. Finally one time I went up to the altar, before communion, and told the Lord that I could not forgive. I gave the whole thing to Him as if I were putting a package in front of Him and asked that He please do it for me.

He did just that. He forgave me and the burden was lifted completely. I learned the joy of forgiveness by His grace.

The relationship with mother was restored and we had at least three good years before she entered eternal rest.

He Gives Us Hope

Chapter 6
THE LIGHT

In 1953 when I had been confirmed in the Episcopal Church the bishop had said, as he laid his hands on my head, "Defend, O Lord, this child with Thy heavenly grace; that she may continue Thine forever; and daily increase in Thy Holy Spirit more and more, until she comes into Thy everlasting kingdom. Amen."

I had at that time received new insights and awareness but on a particular day, the ninth of January, 1958, to be exact, I experienced a revelation very new to me. I know the exact date because I still have the little card Mita gave me with my name, the date, and her initials on it in a place where I keep special mementos.

On that memorable day while I was at home with our children, attending to my household chores, I suddenly had the realization that I was receiving a gift of the Holy Spirit.

I was startled, excited, illumined. I had no idea what it meant or what effect it would have on my life, I just knew it was happening.

My first impulse after the initial awakening was the desire to share with someone. Shark was in class or working and the children were, I felt, too little for me to tell.

Into my mind came the person of Mita, my friend and spiritual mentor, the perfect person to tell. I knew she would understand.

Hurriedly I put on my coat, got my purse and car keys, and told the children I would be right back, feeling that they would be able to take care of each other for fifteen minutes. I then hopped in the car and drove straight to Bairnwick which was only four or five blocks away. I rushed in the back door, which was usually unlocked during the day, and went through the kitchen and hall and upstairs to her room. Somehow I knew I would find her at her desk writing.

There she was, just as I had pictured her in my mind.

I blurted out, "Mita, guess what, I have just received the Holy Spirit."

With my words her face lighted up. She was elated. She understood.

Our encounter was brief and beautiful. I returned to my children and chores. Unfortunately I did not tell Shark. I know not why I was hesitant.

From that moment on I began to have new understanding. Ordinary experiences took on new meaning. I could see reasons for things that had formerly been puzzles to my mind. There were explanations and insights that I had never had before. It was glorious, interesting, fascinating, and exciting, and I soaked it all up like a sponge.

I still cannot tell you what gift of the Holy Spirit I received. I was not concerned with separating and identifying the gifts, rather, I reveled in the new and continuous enlightenment with which I was being blessed.

My attitudes and actions were undoubtedly different toward others. I was able to be more tolerant.

Time passed and our lives were busy.

Shark was working very hard and the children had a series of illnesses. I was a regular, it seemed, at Dr. Ruth Cameron's office. She was a wonderful pediatrician and my good friend.

Chip had a tonsillectomy and then pneumonia, Lucette had bouts with bronchitis, and all four of the children contracted about every virus that came into town.

Ruth discovered that Hilary had one foot and leg turned in, and we were having to make trips to the orthopedic surgeon 60 miles away where she was fitted with one regular and one reverse shoe with a metal bar in between.

The financial struggle was really getting us down, too, as well as all the care required for the little ones.

One day I became very depressed. I was tired, worn out and at my wit's end and just had to get out of the house.

Oftentimes when I felt the need to be alone, I rode out to the Cross on the side of the mountain and sat and prayed at its base until I regained my perspective, but that time I rode around town aimlessly in the car. I don't even remember where I stopped but I pulled over to the side of the road and just sat there.

Suddenly there appeared before my eyes a vision so beautiful and overwhelming that I will never forget it. It is seared even into

He Gives Us Hope

my subconscious and is forever a part of my being.

I saw a bright, bright, light, brighter than anything I had ever seen in my whole life, it was absolutely dazzling!

It was a Presence and I heard a voice saying to me, "I will never leave you. Lo I am with you always even unto the ends of the earth."

I knew it was the Lord.

My life has been different since then, since the visitation to me by the Risen Lord. He has given me a security that no one can ever take away. He is my Light.

All my relationships have been affected by His coming in person to me and by what He said to me.

I love my husband more than ever and can free him to be himself and not hope that he will be "all" to me. Neither do I worry about the inevitable time when he will leave this earthly life to be with our Lord in heaven, should the event precede my time of departure. I know I would miss him terribly but I am not afraid.

The relationships with my children are also enhanced as with my many friends. I can enjoy them for themselves.

I know that He, Jesus the Christ, is the One who will make the difference to others so I try my best to introduce others to Him.

He is the one perfect person, no one else is. We are human beings trying to live in Him.

I trust many others deeply but the one who is completely dependable, always available, and who will never fail you is the Lord Jesus Christ.

What a glorious revelation! I know I will never be alone no matter what circumstances arise. He promised me that, and I know from the Bible and from past experiences that He keeps His promises.

Who am I that the God whom I worship should visit me?

God is gracious. He desires to give us more than we can ever imagine. If we human beings with finite minds could only begin to realize His abounding love and open up to Him we would experience riches beyond our dreams.

I am grateful beyond words.

While still in seminary I began to be asked to give talks to the

Churchwomen in their meetings.

I remember one time ending a talk with the singing of the song, "We are Climbing Jacob's Ladder." Something happened in that room that was way beyond me. The presence of the Lord was there powerfully and beautifully.

After seminary when we lived in nearby Tracy City I was invited in several successive years to speak to the seminary wives. The one thing I stressed was that each young woman would establish a rule of life, and a prayer life of her own. I feel that to be a necessary prerequisite for becoming a successful team when one's husband is a clergyman. Without it the couple has two strikes against them.

I related earlier that we received a scholarship in the form of money for Shark's tuition. We were also awarded a working scholarship at the local grammar school. Since Shark's hours were filled to overflowing we decided that I would be the one to do the required work. The arrangements were made for me to help with remedial reading for one hour a day.

That may sound like a simple assignment but for the Sharkey family it took some split second timing and careful planning in order to fit into our schedules.

As Shark walked in the door from his morning classes I had to walk out and drive down to the school for an hour. He had to be home to take care of the children who were not yet in school. On completion of my hour I had to "hot foot it" back home so that as soon as I returned he could go to his afternoon job. Somewhere in there we all had lunch. It was hectic.

The job was fulfilling and rewarding in that I was able to help some needy little children with problems in their reading.

I had no specific training in the field, but I had been studying for primary education in college, and had been able to help our son Chip over a reading obstacle with which he was confronted. After we had discerned the block, he had sailed ahead.

We carried on the hectic schedule for a while and then one day it all caught up with me.

I became very ill and do not remember at all what my symptoms were, but I do remember that I really honestly thought I was going to die. Why I do not know, and of what I do not remember.

Shark called our doctor and a priest and I was rushed to the hospital.

From the numerous tests that were run the only possible clue to my condition seemed to be that my glucose tolerance test result was "high normal" which indicated that I had a tendency toward diabetes. The doctor gave me a diet and told me that if I did not follow it I would probably be an active diabetic in less than ten years. It was not necessary that I take any medication.

The diagnosis of my condition was "exhaustion." I remained in the hospital for several days, free of any responsibilities, getting ample rest and received from one of the seminary professors, who was a personal friend of Shark's and mine, a sensitive listening ear and the beautiful sacrament of unction for healing.

If one happens to be sick I must say that a seminary locale is a most convenient place to be. Immediately all those connected with the seminary family were alerted, and they were my friends. Single men, married students and their wives, professors and their spouses, all prayed for me and showed evidence of their love and concern.

If you have never been in the position of being the recipient of the combined prayer power of a number of individuals who have the same Lord and the same goals as you, you might not be able to imagine the uplifting, revitalizing force that was in operation. Prayer flowed like a fountain.

My depleted body, mind, and spirit soaked it up like a sponge.

Seminary families do pull together and after I returned home they continued to pray for me and help us out in many ways.

A darling friend, Mary Alice, a very loving and creative person who was a bit bored as she awaited the arrival of her first child, loved coming over to our house to visit. She played with the children, made doll clothes for the girls' dollies, and did ever so many nice things. She was delightful company and afforded welcome adult conversation. I will always remember her help, and especially her joy in giving it.

I was not to continue my job at the grammar school.

I honestly believe it was one of the best things that ever happened to me because from that time on I have tried to not push myself to the brink. When I get very tired I stop if at all possible.

I also found that when I ate the proper foods for my metabolism I felt good, conversely when I ate too many starches or sweets I got tired and felt bad.

I am grateful for the entire episode because though it was very rough, I learned many lessons in the process. It was important. An added benefit was the fact that while I was in the hospital I took the time to write a required paper and answer the questions for my admission in the S.C.H.C.

A beautiful post-script concerning my physical condition occurred approximately fifteen years later. After living with the knowledge of the borderline tendency to diabetes for a decade and a half, the Lord Jesus in His mercy healed me of it.

The healing was made known to me through the following sequence of events.

For a while at that particular time in my life I had felt strongly that the Lord was in the process of doing something very special for me. I had no idea what it was but I did have a real feeling of expectancy.

Of course I had prayed for healing for that infirmity many times, but had never received it.

One summer while Shark was rector of St. Matthias in Nashville, Tennessee, we were on vacation on the Cumberland plateau in Tracy City.

Because Shark had been unable to get a replacement for the early service at St. Matthias, we drove the ninety miles to Nashville just for that one service on a Sunday morning. Only a few people were there.

I was on my knees ready to receive His forgiveness and grace, and when the consecrated bread and wine were given to me His voice spoke to my heart and told me that I didn't have to worry about "that" anymore, it was gone forever.

I knew exactly what He was talking about although I had not been anticipating anything specific that particular day. God surprises us so beautifully. What joy!

As soon as I saw Shark after the service I told him what had

He Gives Us Hope

happened.

We drove back to our property that we called "the Peace of the Rock" for the remainder of our vacation. No longer did I feel suddenly weak and faint when I had used up the energy from the previous meal. I could play tennis, hike, or do any kind of work for a sustained period of time.

Shark could see the difference right away.

Too many sweets or starches at occasional times of splurging did not make me sleepy as they had done before. It was thrilling to feel and know the difference.

On our return to Nashville after vacation I had occasion to see our doctor and during that visit I asked him to please do a blood sugar test on me, as the Red Cross blood bank was scheduled to come to our church and I wanted to be a donor. I had not been able to do that previously because of the diabetic tendency.

When Morse read the test results he said, "Certainly you may give blood, your test is completely clear."

I told him what had happened and he, being a beautiful Christian, understood and shared my elation. I went on my way rejoicing.

There had been no medical treatment involved in my healing, only the intervention of a loving God who continues to heal through His Son Jesus.

Chapter 7
YOU CAN'T PUT GOD IN A BOX

Allow me to digress for a moment more, from the chronological development of my story, to open the door a little wider on the wonders of God's grace exemplified in the magnificent splendor of the ministry of spiritual healing and the life of the Spirit.

It was in that first eventful year in seminary that I had begun to learn a smattering of the reality and beauty of that portion of the gospel, God's power to heal.

He told His disciples to heal as well as preach and teach and to cast out demons in His name. Jesus is the same yesterday, today, and forever.

The seminary brought in guest lecturers from time to time. One such seminar featured the Reverend and Mrs. Edgar Sanford, those great proponents of the ministry of spiritual healing who spearheaded the movement in the Episcopal Church when it was weak.

Some of the other seminary wives I knew were not at all interested and were very skeptical. They did not want to attend the lectures and talked about those "way out" people, or some such misnomer, but I wanted to go and did.

I had always wanted to really believe the miracles in the Bible and had heard of miraculous occurrences in modern times, but skepticism is rampant among clergy and lay people alike as it is among atheists and agnostics, and I had been exposed to that sort of harangue so I was not absolutely sure.

"Lord, I believe; help thou my unbelief" (Mark 9:24 KJV).

At the opening of the lectures Edgar spoke first and was excellent, forthright, strong in his faith and knowledgeable in the subject. He spoke with power and authority. What I heard made sense to me and struck a chord that felt right.

Agnes Sanford delivered the next lecture. She too was an excellent speaker. I got on the same wave length with her that evening and heard her every word and intonation.

All they revealed about their own God-given healings and the numerous examples they cited from their lives fascinated me.

After I heard them I was convinced!

Shark and I began our journey into that magnificent land and have lived in it ever since. In later years we have been privileged to also hear and read the works of many others on the subject, including most of the books by Edgar and Agnes Sanford.

Emily Gardiner Neal, the skeptic turned advocate, who wrote the book "A Reporter Finds God Through Spiritual Healing" and many more, was a champion in the ministry of spiritual healing. We have heard her speak and own most of her books, too.

Morton Kelsey, priest, teacher, and author is powerful and authoritative as well as witty and is a spellbinding lecturer.

Dr. Alfred Price, who for years was the warden of the Order of St. Luke the Physician, the interdenominational international organization devoted to the ministry of spiritual healing, and of which Shark and I have been members for years, is our friend and has conducted healing missions in our various churches at three different times. We have sat at his feet in our living room after his lectures enthralled as he dropped pearls of wisdom and experience.

Francis McNutt has written one of the most comprehensive books (in my estimation) that I have read on the subject. It is entitled, "Healing." He and his wife, Judith, have written several others.

Mark Pearson is another good author, speaker, and teacher.

There are many more too numerous to list, but most all good.

The field of spiritual healing deals with the whole person, body, mind, and spirit.

Along with the healing described in the previous chapter the Lord has blessed me with others.

I have received a "new ear" by means of eardrum grafts, at the hands of skillful Christian surgeons, forty years after my hearing had been impaired as a child by constant ear infections, and again when scar tissue had built up and additional surgery was called for. It was indeed exciting one year to be able to tell my friends that I had received a new ear for Christmas, a unique gift and one for which I was especially grateful. My hearing has been restored to being almost normal, when I previously could only hear about half in my right ear.

High blood pressure used to plague me until a chain of events led me to a new doctor.

A call my husband received to a church in a different state meant a move for us and of course different doctors in the new locale.

To my delight one fine Christian doctor, highly trained and sensitive, felt that a medicine I was taking that had been prescribed for me years before (and one that has since been found to have harmful side effects for some people) was likely to be a heavy contributor to my having high blood pressure. I was actually there for a gynecological checkup. He took me off the prescription under careful supervision, before he stopped the blood pressure medicine, and saw that my blood pressure was normal. Then he had me stop taking both, checked me and found that it was still normal.

I could have jumped up in his lap I was so thrilled. Together we rejoiced in the discovery.

Physicians, surgeons, ministers, Christian psychiatrists, nurses, counselors, lay people who care and believe, are all used by God when they open themselves up to be used as instruments of God's healing power.

Some healings are instantaneous, others happen over an extended period of time. There is no certain prescription, there are no pat answers. He never ceases to amaze and excite me.

Through a friend by the name of Elsie I learned that God the Creator desires to, and continues to, create and renew His creatures.

I met Elsie at a conference at Adelynrood (the summer home of the S.C.H.C.) one summer in the sixties. Arriving there tired, physically and spiritually, while walking around the beautiful grounds before dinner my steps fell in rhythm with and alongside Elsie.

She was warm, friendly, gracious, and vibrant. We began talking.

I told Elsie that I was very tired and so glad to be there, that I really needed rest and refreshment and that I had come to the conference with a real sense of expectancy. She beamed forth understanding.

At dinner things began to happen. God was in the process of feeding both my body and mind and certainly my spirit. In His

He Gives Us Hope

world of nature, through the sacraments, in communal worship, and fellowship the potential is infinite.

He started as He often does with people being His instruments. That time they were Companions of the Holy Cross. Conversations, looks, handshakes, smiles, sharing at the evening meal, were all part of the ongoing recreating experience.

Evening Prayer and Compline, beautiful evening worship services, were particularly meaningful to me that night and I really had a good sleep.

The next day's program commenced with the Holy Communion, when our Blessed Lord comes to His people in a special way. He bestowed on this child of His, me, an additional portion of the bounty of His grace.

He was smiling on me and showing me His love.

The morning was glorious. It was cool, fresh, and the birds were singing their beautiful songs. The flowers in the gardens were luxuriant with color and fragrance. I was indeed happy to be alive.

I saw Elsie after breakfast and told her that the Lord had blessed me with some beautiful gifts and that I felt much better, very much in fact, and thanked her for her prayers.

Then she said something very startling. At least it was to me, it was new to my ears.

She said that when the Lord began giving me blessings, one after another, not to cut Him off, but to let the blessings keep coming!

I realized that I had been close to doing just that! With some very special expressions of His love I had been ready to say "thank you" to Him and think that He was finished, that He had given me enough.

Looking quizzically at Elsie I asked her if she really meant it and she reassured me that she did.

That lovely lady, I found out, had been involved in the ministry of healing for years. She knew of God's goodness and bounty, that He does not just put a "band aid" on our wounds and hurts but heals them deep down, and all the way, if we let Him.

I am still grateful for her words of wisdom and counsel because throughout the entire conference I received pearl after pearl of His infinite riches and grace.

Needless to say I returned home to my family revitalized and ready to tackle the next hurdles of my life as they were to emerge.

I have seen God heal in so many different ways it is magnificent and awe-inspiring. You can't put God in a box!

A number of years ago, at another S.C.H.C. conference at Adelynrood, a friend of mine told the group that her eyesight was deteriorating, that she was facing surgery, and asked for our prayers. I felt led to respond, not only in silent prayer but in action, and when I saw her later that day asked if I might have a prayer with her. She was very pleased and agreed to my offer.

We stopped right then and there under the arbor going to the chapel and prayed. As I held her hands in mine I asked Almighty God to heal her eyes, to guide the hands of the surgeon as he operated, and then the next words that issued from my mouth (and I knew that they were not mine) were that "she might see with the eyes of Christ." She and I were both somewhat surprised. She was grateful.

We saw each other sometime later at another conference and Virginia came up to me and told me the wonderful things that had happened to her. She said that she did have the surgery, which was successful, that her eyesight was much improved, but before that an amazing transformation had taken place. She found that she was feeling much more compassion for people and was much more accepting and patient with others than she had been before. Virginia was truly pleased and we both acknowledged that the Lord had indeed answered the prayer that He had brought forth through my mouth and hands when I had prayed for her.

Mildred, another friend, had a tumor on her bladder that, when biopsied, proved to be cancerous. She had deep faith and felt the Lord could really heal her, and would if she asked Him, but had some trepidation that her faith might not be strong enough.

When she told me that I replied that the healing did not depend on the amount of her faith, it depended on the fact and knowledge that God does want to and is able to heal. I added that He knew how much faith she had and would use that, plus the faith of others who prayed for her. A lot of people feel that they don't have enough (and

60   He Gives Us Hope

that makes them feel guilty, which is no help at all). Others have not much knowledge of God's healing power but can depend on the faith of those who are willing to pray for them and are aware of how loving God is. I prayed for her, as did many others, and laid hands on her.

Mildred had the surgery, the tumor was contained and was easily removed, and she went through chemotherapy and radiation with a minimum amount of discomfort, much less than most people seem to experience. We had remembered her and lifted her up in prayer whenever she had the treatments.

She healed, with no traces of the cancerous tissues anywhere and is a powerful witness, very willingly open, testifying to others, when occasions present themselves, of God's healing power.

He can even heal our memories. God has healed many bad memories in my life with the help of the prayers and love of others in Jesus' name.

Having one's memories healed is not like having amnesia. God does not erase the facts and conditions surrounding our hurts. If He did that He would be removing a portion of our life experiences, which are all part and parcel of our being who we are.

God removes the hurts, stings, and blows I have felt. I still remember that I did hurt, but that awful feeling in the pit of my stomach, the lump in my throat when I think of the experience again, is gone. He instead gives me some positive emotions.

He is still healing my memories of things that happened years ago as different episodes arise to my conscious mind from time to time and are dealt with. Jesus is there with me in the midst of my memory and He helps me forgive or accept forgiveness and He takes the pain away that was caused by traumas that were from circumstances beyond my control, the ones in which I was an innocent victim.

He will continue to heal more memories when I ask Him, as there will be fresh hurts since I am vulnerable and take risks. I will make more mistakes because I am a human being. It is wonderful to know that the God whom I worship and adore is ready, willing, and able to "keep the slate clean" and heal me anew with fresh anointings.

Because of the remembrance of traumas in our lives, particularly if they have been the result of our failures, we learn not to make the same mistakes again. Plus the fact that they give us the added dimension of being able to empathize with and understand more fully those we know and pray for who are going through similar traumatic experiences. God uses me quite frequently in that capacity.

The more we give to others the more we receive.

While we were in our first church in Tracy City, we attended a Bryan Green crusade in Chattanooga, Tennessee, when at the "invitation," very much like that at a Billy Graham crusade, I arose from my seat in the back of the auditorium and went down to rededicate my life to Christ and His work. Praise God. Good things happen at those when one does it sincerely.

Another happened in the 70s when Shark and I attended one of Agnes Sanford's Schools of pastoral Care at Dubose Conference

Connie's painting of Jesus "Come Unto Me"

He Gives Us Hope

Center at which time we asked for the baptism of the Holy Spirit. That was powerful and again we were filled with the Spirit and I felt that I received one of the gifts of the Holy Sprit, the gift of healing. That is to say, healing for myself plus the ability to be used as an instrument of God's healing power to heal those for whom I would pray when led to do so. This is an awesome gift, as they all are, and I am deeply humbled. It is not in my power, it has nothing to do with me, except that I am a willing and hopefully open conduit for God to work through. Ever since then it has been an important part of my ministry, especially after we were inducted into the order of St. Luke, the international interdenominational order for spiritual and physical healing. At that time our hands were anointed with oil for the purpose of laying on of hands for healing. We had to take instruction before receiving the anointing and induction.

At the time of the baptism of the Holy Spirit, I did not receive the gift of tongues (glossalalia), though I had wished for it. At a later date I was re-reading the book by Dennis Bennett entitled, "Nine o'clock in the Morning." In it Dennis talked about the gift of tongues among other things.

So it happened one New Year's Eve. We were scheduled to go to a party with a number or couples from St. Matthias in Nashville, and Shark was unexpectedly called out to help with a parishioner who was an alcoholic and his family was having a big problem with him that night. Oh phooey! Many times our plans were altered at the last minute by some emergency and I knew Shark had to go, so off he went.

I was by myself, so I went down into our den downstairs and sitting on the sofa read some more of "Nine o'clock in the Morning." It was then that Dennis said, in essence, that if you have asked for the gift of tongues and have not received it, ask again. So I did just that. He suggested how to proceed and I did as he said, and lo and behold, it came! Slowly a few sounds which I did not recognize as anything I knew or was familiar with emerged. I stopped and started again and the same syllables came again and again. Not many, but definitely the same and unintelligible to me. Some people who do not know about glossalalia think you can't stop and start at will, but you can.

I was so excited and very awed by the experience and wondered if it was the real thing. I knew very well from reading, that all the gifts of the Spirit have counterfeits and I surely did not want to have that. To test it, the next day I called my good friend, Anne Murphy, another clergy wife whose husband was rector of the Episcopal Church closest to us in Nashville, and asked if I could come and see her and pray with her. We prayed and shared periodically, another experience for which I am deeply grateful. Anne said "Yes" and asked me to come on over that day. I went and told her what had happened and she was happy for me and suggested we pray together in English first and then let the Spirit take over. We did. Anne began, then I prayed and she started praying in tongues, then I followed and the same sounds issued from my mouth that had come on New Year's Eve. We prayed a short while, then Anne said, "Why Connie, you have a beautiful prayer language!" (That's what most people call it.) John Sherrill has a beautiful little book called, "They Speak with Other Tongues" that explains some history about the use of the gift with many amazing stories. I have used the gift a lot, especially when praying for others (usually silently unless I know that they understand the gift), as well as in my private prayers. The person does not know what I am saying, nor do I, but God does. It is the Spirit in me speaking to God's Spirit.

I do not believe that the gift is a prerequisite of someone's having the Holy Spirit, as I know a number of people who manifest many gifts of the Spirit and do not have that one, to feel that to be true. I felt that maybe it was given to me so that I know it is valid, and because I was in the habit of speaking to many individuals about the spiritual life and so I would be able to tell others about it, especially if they asked or were skeptical or afraid, as many people are.

I know it transcends any personality conflict or clash, and it penetrates any evil spirit that may be lurking, for as I said, it goes directly from Spirit to Spirit. It has been a blessing and I praise God for it.

Chapter 8
ALL WORK AND NO PLAY
MAKES THEOLOGS DULL

We had a lot of fund during the three years in seminary. The men who entered with Shark in the fall of 1957 made up a very closely knit group along with the families of those who were married. Nearly fifty-eight percent of all the "theologs" when we were there had been formerly in some form of business or non-religious occupations ("retreads" Shark likes to call them) and the majority of that group were married and had families. At age 36 Shark thought he would possibly be the "old man," but found that to be not at all the case. We were also surprised that there were a number of families with four children as we had. The single men were for the most part right out of college.

An interesting observation about human nature, and the pride that sometimes enters in and how God deals with it, was beautifully exemplified in the following experience.

When we "left our nets and followed Him" (our secure jobs and comfortable homes and environments) we were at times "puffed up" and sort of patting ourselves on the back for being so great.

Those balloons were soon punctured and the wind quickly taken out of the sails when we got to seminary and came in contact with all those other families who had done the same thing. We saw we weren't extra special at all, and were cut down to size and given perspective. When we realized it we laughed about it. God was smiling, too, I'm sure.

The class had periodic get togethers, cookouts, and parties at the home of one or another of us who had enough room for the whole gang. Those really helped break the tension that naturally builds up in academic life, particularly under the rigors of graduate level work. Between heavy assignment loads, divergent personalities, financial binds, often closely cramped quarters for families, and unwelcome dormitory style life for single men, some change of pace and shift of scene was needed for everyone. The parties were occasions of real conviviality.

Yearly on St. Luke's day each new class of theologs had to work up and present a funny skit as a part of the evening's program. Some were hilarious.

Since St. Luke's day comes in October the exchange of ideas, the planning, practices, and eventual presentation of the skits contribute greatly to the initial phase of molding each class into a group, plus tending to take the starch out of stuffed shirts.

Shark and I took part also, later in our first year, in an historical pageant depicting the life of the University of the South which has a long and rich heritage.

The setting of our small part was a gala ball at which we waltzed rhythmically around the stage accompanied by about a dozen other couples, also residents of Sewanee, all splendidly bedecked in authentic costumes of the period. Along with being lots of fun it enabled us to get acquainted with other residents of Sewanee who were not in seminary, some connected with the University, and some townspeople.

The lives of our children consisted of typical activities such as Cub Scouts for Chip, Brownies for Lucette, playing with the neighbors and other friends, playing on the swing set in the back yard, birthday parties, and Lucette's initiation into the feat of cheerleading for her grammar school room.

Hilary, being the youngest, was lonely when Chip and Lucette went off to regular school and Griff attended nursery school. Not wanting to be excluded from conversations involving the framework of classes and teachers, she invented her own. She ingeniously came up with a teacher named "Mrs. Kimber," complete with family. This imaginary lady had two children, a girl named "Deborah New Orleans" pronounced Debra New Orleens, and a boy named "Hosper." Hilary would delight us with tales of their escapades, joining the other children in what amounted to "show and tell time" at meals or in the evenings. We all went along with her fantasy just as surely as if Mrs. Kimber and her offspring had been flesh and blood persons, even to the point of setting places at the table for them at tea parties.

One day, out of the blue, right before she was to start kindergarten, little Hilary calmly announced very seriously that Mrs. Kimber and her children were moving to California; thus their exit from the scene and the world of her environment, never to be spoken of again. The other kids were so good about it and needless to say the Kimber trio are treasured in the storehouse of family memorabilia.

Another form of diversion was for the single men to come to our home, usually one or two at a time. They felt relaxed and comfortable with our family.

I like to cook and am lucky to have a family who thoroughly enjoys eating and it is usually plausible to put another plate on the table and stretch the food a bit. I also totally believe in the "loaves and fishes" and somehow when one does believe, it does work! (Church covered dish suppers are a splendid example.)

We often exchanged a home cooked meal for babysitting. That arrangement was gratifying for all concerned. The men naturally got tired of institutional fare and appreciated what we had to offer, plus the fact that they loved our four little children. Having young men as sitters was a treat to the kids, in fact they really preferred them to having the girls who came to sit occasionally. Because we had children of varying ages there was always one who could tell the "visiting fireman" where anything was located or what family customs and procedures were. Of course, as youngsters do with any substitute, they tried to pull the wool over their eyes with pranks and mischief, but that was part of the fun.

When one particular young gentleman came the kids would invariably initiate the game of throwing one child at a time up in the air by holding the four corners of a stout blanket and tossing with gusto. Our kids still talk about that when we reminisce. In fact they can gleefully remember all sorts of schemes and games that were devised and reveled in when the boys were there. We were happy for them and Shark and I were getting out of the house and away from our responsibilities for a respite. All of us who are parents know how that helps one's nerves and perspective and consequently our marriages.

Of the four or five who came fairly regularly each said that the children behaved quite well and they always wanted an invitation to return. When all was quiet and the children were bedded down, Ben Shawhan, Dick Bass, John Bell, Phil Whitehead, and Ben Hunter (whom one of the kids called "Ben Tunter"), whichever was there, delved into his studies in front of the fire until we came home. When we returned we often had a drink and a bit of a chat with them.

Dick particularly relished my blue cheese dressing for salads. I can still envision him, with his blonde flat top hair cut, sitting in our kitchen with the family, helping himself to another portion of salad and raving about my dressing. One night when dinner was over he looked up with imploring eyes and asked rather hesitatingly if I minded if he ate the rest of the dressing, he loved the taste of it so well. I was a bit startled, but pleased, and told him that he could certainly have it, whereupon he gobbled up all that was left with epicurean delight.

A professor, a bachelor, frequently included our home in the itinerary of his afternoon walk. He was on a stringent diet and when I found out that lamb patties were among the few items allowed him, I almost always bought a few and tucked them in a corner of the freezer in the eventuality that Dr. Sauerbrei chose to bless us with his presence.

He was a delightful man and had a wealth of fascinating stories which he loved to tell over a cup of tea. Claude Sauerbrei had been born in the Canary Islands, I believe educated in England (he had a beautiful British accent), had come to this country and at that time was teaching Old Testament in the seminary. He was particularly enamored of Hilary. As he did not drive, occasionally I acted as chauffeur if he had an errand to do, with one-year-old Hilary sitting in the car seat between our approximately fifty-year-old friend and me. Hilary derived pleasure from the outing and the good Doctor's attention. One day he looked over at her and said beguilingly, "You gray-eyed beauty, I would like to wait for you to grow up," I was so amused because he said it so seriously.

For dessert Dr. Sauerbrei could have bananas, and that was about all. The first time I had the pleasure of serving him dinner I fretted nervously, not knowing what might be the most ladylike way to serve a banana for dessert to a gentleman of culture. Should I

He Gives Us Hope

peel it and put it on a plate, cut it up and serve it in a dish or what? I finally decided to unaffectedly hand him the fruit "au natural," peel and all! Don't we human beings get in a dither over silly things?

I was careful in my buying of food, and by the grace of God we never missed a meal, and had enough to share with our guests. But one episode that we really fretted over concerning food and finances, that wasn't silly at all, occurred when a new semester was about to begin.

According to University rules one could not register if he had any unpaid bills on campus. We bought many of our groceries and all needed medicines from the University Supply Store to whom we owed a sizable sum.

We had no money left in the bank, the Bishop was in England at the time of the Lambeth Conference so we could not ask him for money, the Dean had none available, our scholarship funds were expended and we were about at the end of our ropes. There was one more day before registration.

As was his usual custom, Shark went to the post office to pick up our mail and there in our box was a check for $500.00 from a church in Knoxville, St. John's. They thought we might be in need!

The next day we were solvent, Shark was registered for the next semester and we knew God and His people cared and that He wanted us to go on.

Mildred McGee was one of my favorite people. She was a very pretty lady with lovely wavy silver gray hair which was always well groomed. Her clothes were conservative but stylish and she was peppy, witty, very gentle, and to me the personification of the word LOVE. You could just feel it when you were in her presence. We met at an S.C.H.C. chapter meeting in Sewanee as she was a Companion.

Mildred had formerly lived in that beautiful town on the mountain, was a close friend of Mita's and in fact had taught in Mita's school at Bairnwick. She had moved back to Mississippi, her home state, then after her children were grown and married, had returned to Sewanee. In her late fifties when we became friends, I found her to be a lady generously endowed with wisdom from on high.

Mildred had lived through some very rough times in her life and she shared the trauma of some of them with me. Her trust in me, a much younger woman, was very touching. We have cried together as well as laughed many times and I loved her dearly. The last time I was with her she was somewhat crippled up with arthritis in her knees but did not allow that malady to dull her wit, love, and joie de vivre.

It was she who led me unafraid through the inevitable change of life. Instead of the old wives' tales I had heard of the awful times some women have, she told me that just as a young girl grows into puberty and her body changes slowly and naturally, so do we slowly and naturally change in later life, that it is God's process for women and He takes care of it. Because of her telling me that I experienced what she had predicted and have tried to pass that information on to other young women who are approaching that time of life with trepidation.

Mildred had a raft of funny stories which she told in her very Southern accent. Most had as their locale the small Mississippi town where she had grown up. One of my favorites was her anecdote concerning a young lady who had not been fully endowed with gray matter, and for whom everyone who knew her got out of her way when she drove her automobile around the village. One day a stranger was driving through town and stopped at a crossroad, whereupon the weak-minded one drove up behind him and slammed her car right into the back end of his. When he hopped out of his car and angrily confronted her with the question of why she had not stopped or blown her horn but had run into him, she replied with exasperation, "Well, I said Oogie Oogie"!

We were fortunate in having, on the outskirts of Sewanee, a small picturesque lake we often frequented for swimming and picnics. It was an avenue of escape from the humdrum, where mothers met and exchanged chit chat as well as affording them fun and relaxation along with their small fry.

I was there one day with my little brood and to my delight found Mildred on the beach sunbathing. We spread our beach towels and blankets near hers. Pretty soon along came a seminary wife, whom I knew, with her two charges. We exchanged greetings and

　　　　　　　　He Gives Us Hope

she plunked herself down near our post, then began a harangue about how much she had to do at home, what a bother it was to bring the children out, how she wished she were at home accomplishing what was left undone there, and generally grumbling about everything under the sun.

When the "grouch" went out to the water with her children Mildred leaned over to me and said,"She might just as well have stayed home. She's not doing any good for anyone, least of all her children, with an attitude like that and she's putting a damper on everyone else's fun, to boot!"

That bit of wisdom struck me very poignantly. I have tried to keep in my mind since then, "Work while you work and play while you play. Forget your burdens and leave them home when you're out for fun."

It was Mildred who first brought to my attention the adage that "Beauty is in the eyes of the beholder." I believe that to be true. Just as "Miracles happen to those who look for them."

Speaking of miracles, the last year at Sewanee a group from our church in Norris, St. Francis, spearheaded by Bill Pollard, started a fund named "H.S.T.S." (Help Sharkey Through Seminary) to which they each pledged a certain monthly sum. The check was sent to us every month at school and the donors remained anonymous.

Our children recognized the fact that people were concerned and were sharing their worldly goods with us. This was particularly evident on one occasion which is vivid in Shark's and my memories.

The House of Young Churchmen was meeting at DuBose, our diocesan conference center, and our priest, Hank Myers, was their leader. He told them about the struggle our family was having to get through seminary and on the last day of the conference they voted to designate their offering as a gift to the Sharkey family.

Hank and a few of the young people brought the money to us at our home in a brown paper grocery bag, out of which he proceeded to pour the contents onto the coffee table in our living room in the presence of the whole family. It was indeed a gift of love. I feel that Hank showed real insight in doing it that way rather than converting the money into check form because there on the table was

He Gives Us Hope   71 ninety dollars in nickels, dimes, pennies, and quarters, the kind of money with which our little children could identify. They were overwhelmed and said in awed tones, "These people care that much about us?" We were all dissolved in tears of love, joy, and gratitude.

We had many good times while we were in Sewanee while Shark was studying for the priesthood. Occasionally when things got tense and Shark had tons of work to do for exams or required papers, the children and I took off and visited friends or family so that he could have peace and quiet.

Seminary families are a close lot, having so much in common, there is among them a real camaraderie. You have heard it said, "How those Christians love one another!" I think it is probably because "He hath set His love upon me" (Psalm 91:14).

He Gives Us Hope

Chapter 9
OUT POTTED PALM

It happened on Ash Wednesday. The snow was coming down continuously, a heavy blanket, covering everything in sight. Then the rain commenced and the temperature took a sudden drop.

The men, the seminarians, were on their Lenten retreat at DuBose, the conference center several miles down the road. They were not due to return to their homes until late that day, but because the weather was getting increasingly mean and the roads treacherous, someone in charge had the good sense to dismiss them early. It seemed expedient that wives and children should no longer be by themselves.

Upon Shark's arrival home, together we took inventory of the resources on hand in the event of a power failure. Just about everything in our home operated on electricity, the stove, refrigerator, lights of course, and wall heaters. We were blessed with a wood burning fireplace and plenty of wood so we knew that we could have some degree of warmth in one part of the house, and we could also cook in a limited way, and heat water or soup.

Shark assessed the situation and decided we had better have a kerosene stove or two if we could find them, so he proceeded to go down to the village in search of them and any other supplies he could find, which would be necessary or helpful to our situation.

Before he left we determined that our four children and I should be together in one spot. We chose the hide-a-bed in the living room located right in front of the fireplace. The glowing friendly fire added coziness and warmth and along with our "togetherness" helped dispel our apprehension and anxiety. Besides that, because of the structure of the house, that particular room had a second story above it and would afford further protection. Limbs were snapping off like toothpicks and we could hear ominous sounds outside as the freezing rain continued to fall and envelope each twig in its heavy burdensome snare of ice.

Chip, Lucette, Griff, Hilary, and I told stories, read books, played games, and really had a pretty good time as the seconds and minutes ticked by.

Then suddenly we heard a thundering crash followed by shattering of glass. Somewhere, something had hit in very close proximity to the five of us, we knew not where.

When the noise had ceased and we had somewhat collected our composure, we ventured off our perch on the hide-a-bed in the direction of the sounds. Someone found the "victim" glass, the light fixture in the bathroom, which had been dislodged from its peace and quiet and had fallen to the floor, broken into a thousand pieces. Without yet bothering with the cleanup operation but with stern warnings that no one was to go near it, we thought we had better hazard a look into the room directly above the bathroom.

There in the children's playroom were two branches sticking through the roof looking very ugly and treacherous, but with no apparent accompanying damage. After assessing the situation in the other room, which was the children's dormitory style bedroom, and finding nothing alarming there, we breathed signs of relief and went back downstairs. We cleaned up the mess in the bathroom and then resumed our chosen place of safety, the friendly hide-a-bed in front of the fire, while we awaited Shark's return.

As soon as he came in the door, resplendent with two kerosene stoves and their necessary components, the children bombarded him with the tale of the calamity. I am sure I added to the description but my feeling was mostly one of relief that "Daddy" was back home safely and the whole family was again all together.

Shortly thereafter Shark went into his office a room in the back of the house on the same floor as the living room, whereupon he came racing back to us with his mouth flapping open and closed, unable to speak, and his hand pointing in the direction of his office.

We all charged from our perches and followed him to find a huge tree probably a foot in circumference going right through the middle of the room. Insulation, ice, snow, and dirt were everywhere. What a mess!

The tree top had snapped off and plummeted like a spear through the ceiling, completely through the room, and stopped only after piercing the floor. The intruders in the upstairs room were smaller branches from the same tree, all connected.

He Gives Us Hope

I can still remember our amazement as we starred incredulously at the bizarre scene. Hilary was only three years old and she was the one who first spoke, wide eyed, saying, "Oh my goodness!" That statement has its

place in the repertoire of family classics.

We were indeed grateful. No one had been hurt, not one piece of furniture had been damaged. The tree missed the three quarter bed in the room, the desk, the chair, and barely dented Shark's typewriter. It had gone through the floor at a point just missing the rug, and the electrical wiring between the floors and ceilings had not been disturbed. It was as if the hand of the Lord had guided that object of destruction to completely protect us and cause the least possible damage. If the wires had been hit we could easily have had a fire on our hands, too. We did not.

Shark decided that we must leave as there were many more such large trees surrounding the house, and by then the power was cut off since many electrical lines had been torn down all over town.

We were not sure where to go. Who could suddenly and without any warning absorb a family of six and a dog for an indefinite period of time? Then Shark got the brilliant idea–DuBose, where he had just been.

Luckily we still had a telephone connection so he promptly called Monteagle and asked Winnie and Ernie (the superintendent and his wife who were our close friends) if we could possibly come there.

They said "sure" that there were already about five other families who had preceded us in coming.

In a scurry and flutter of activity we rounded up what we could think of that we would need in the way of clothes, et cetera, and what food we had on hand that could be prepared easily. Suitcases were filled with much excitement and it became rather an adventure after we recovered from the initial shock.

Before leaving we had to figure out some way to keep the elements from continually destroying our back room where the tree was lodged. We found a huge piece of plastic and somehow tacked it to the ceiling, over the

bed, to afford a little temporary protection to the furniture. There was no place, nor any time to move it. We had to get out of there as quickly as possible, while the road between Sewanee and Monteagle was still traversable.

Upon our arrival at DuBose we carted all our gear into the dormitory, finding adjoining rooms on the hall so we could be close to each other. Shark and I took one room, the two girls a second and the two boys a third. As there was no heat in the building we went

He Gives Us Hope

to the supply room and acquired a large supply of blankets. We could keep warm at night by piling them on. Bathrooms were available and usable, but cold. The one warm room and the brightest spot in the whole building was the huge "common room" at one end of the building. A blazing fire in the enormous fireplace heated and cheered the entire room and its occupants.

We joined the four or five other families of seminarians from Sewanee who had already arrived, several of whom had mattresses sprawled on the floor as they had babies who couldn't be left in the corridor rooms. There was a real feeling of camaraderie and most seemed to really be having a good time together and of a certainty making the most of an unusual and undesirable predicament.

You have heard the expression, "If you get a lemon, make lemonade!" We did.

A common enemy makes for unity and the group became harmonious as we shared our common trials and thanksgivings.

Several families had the foresight to bring charcoal grills which were set up in operation in parts of the hall. They could not be used in the common room because of the fumes. On the grills we cooked appropriate foods until a day or so later we were able to do some cooking in the kitchen. I presume the kitchen must have had other than electrical appliances. I don't remember that part.

The scene outside the next day was diabolically beautiful. Virtually a fairyland, the trees and bushes sparkled and glowed in the sunlight like so many diamonds, each twig and branch producing its own facet to reflect the gorgeous colors of the spectrum from the sun's rays, sky, clouds, and landscape.

The diabolical character of the picture made it tempting and inviting to investigate with no evident foreboding of its potential treachery. Such is the way of the tempter Satan. He tries to entice and lure us into situations that look so desirous and full of delight, while giving no warning of the possible dire circumstances one can encounter if he enters the arena of fascination. He loves to try to trap us.

We were aware of the dangers outside so we had to keep the children and a few adventuresome adults from venturing into that never-neverland. In order to do that, we devised interesting activities inside. The children had a ball, releasing pent up energy by racing back and forth down the long corridors, playing tag and hide and seek in the rooms, and exploring. I really don't recall any great problems. The conference center was not in regular use and we had the place to ourselves, so it was the entire group who made the rules.

We chatted, sang, prayed, played games, ate, slept, and took care of our children for the four or five days we were there. There was much sharing of stories of why and how the Lord had called each of the men and their families to seminary.

One day was particularly meaningful when a priest came and celebrated the Holy Communion for us in the common room. With mattresses, babies, and the whole works in that one large room we shared in a truly moving Eucharist; Eucharist means thanksgiving.

Eventually the men ventured back to Sewanee when we found that the power had been restored to parts of the town, each man going to his own bailiwick to ascertain if it were yet safe for families to return to their homes. After holing up at DuBose and being very grateful for the temporary lodging given us when we had been driven out of our homes we, the Sharkey family, went back to the "Tennessee House," as it had been named, or "Gailor Cottage," as most people in town knew it.

When we hired a man to come and cut the trees "up/down?" He laughed and laughed, and when we questioned him about what was so funny he told us, "I've cut down many a tree in my time, but this is the first one I've ever cut down in a house!"

Our family chucklingly refers to the tree as our "potted palm." Repairs were made to the house and life went on.

He Gives Us Hope

Chapter 10
VIGNETTES OF A CLERGY FAMILY

In the spring of 1960 as graduation approached there was a stir of excitement and anticipation. Where was each man going to serve the Lord? What would the church look like, the town, the people who make up the church, what would be their way of life? It's like waiting for a baby to be born.

The Bishop of the diocese from which every seminarian comes has the prerogative of placing his charges in the locale that he deems best for all concerned.

Some who might be suitable for eventual team ministries, or those who are likely to prefer and be most at home in large parish churches, and need to learn the ropes, are sent as deacons in training, under the supervision of men with the capabilities of teaching and advising, or as assistants in large churches which require a staff of more than one clergyman.

Another category is that of the small churches. Those assigned to such cures are sometimes young men who seem to have a good bit of initiative and leadership qualities, ingenuity and vision, or the more mature men, with the aforementioned attributes, who have had the experience out in the world and will be able to pull together and help develop those groups into being cohesive congregations. Hopefully those churches will move in direction of parish status (if they have not yet reached it) that is to say, toward being self-supporting. In some cases the men in rural areas serve more than one mission church, oftentimes in situations or areas that have limited growth potential but are nonetheless strong important bulwarks of the faith, many having been in existence for decades.

The Bishops do their best to insure proper fit, and refrain from putting square pegs in round holes and vice versa. I am grateful to be able to say that the families of the clergymen are also taken into consideration in the deliberations.

In the Episcopal Church, after that initial placing by the Bishop, and after a man has been a deacon for a period of six months to a year and then ordained priest (at which time he receives the privilege and authority to administer the sacraments) he may then accept or reject calls from other churches or dioceses. That is, of course, contingent upon the permission of the Bishops of both dioceses, and after prayerful consideration as to where the priest feels the Lord wants him at that time. There is no "usual" or prescribed length of tenure.

Shark's experience and personality are more compatible with the small town ministry. Our preference has been for living in smaller communities near cities, rather than in metropolitan areas, though we have served in both settings.

As a seminarian, Shark held services and worked with the young people at Christ Church, Tracy City, Tennessee, which is fourteen miles down the road from Sewanee, on that portion of the Cumberland plateau. The church had been there for years and had a small but faithful congregation who were at that time without a priest. They have by now celebrated their one hundred-twenty-third anniversary and we were privileged to attend the festive centennial celebration a number of years ago.

That group of dedicated Christians requested of the Bishop that Shark be sent to them as their minister and we were delighted that their request was granted, as Shark really wanted to serve the Lord there.

When the school year rolled around and the course work was completed, then came the grueling three days of oral and written canonical examinations preparatory to ordination. After that ordeal Shark was graduated from the seminary and received a Bachelor of Divinity degree from the University of the South. In later years that degree has been chanced to a Masters of Divinity and the school granted to all alumni holding Bachelors the higher Masters degrees.

The children were as proud of their father as I was of my husband. He had worked hard indeed to attain that goal. We had gone through a lot, as I have recounted in this partial disclosure of our lives there. We had taken a leap of faith to go and had learned faith while we were going through it.

A lady in Knoxville had posed the question to me prior to our entering the seminary experience, "Connie, do you think you can take it?" Her question had startled me, but I honestly didn't resent

He Gives Us Hope

it. She was right, could I take it? Somehow I had felt I could. I had known it would be a big challenge, and I certainly had no idea whatsoever what would be in store for the Sharkey family, but we had been willing to go forward and to trust in God, who had called us.

I am really grateful that we were advised to go the regular route and not as Shark had first wanted, as a two-year special student,

because I believe it took the full three years for me to make the transition from one kind of life to that of being a minister's wife.

I would like to say that I dearly love the role of being the wife of an Episcopal priest. I wouldn't change places with anybody else for a million dollars. It is rewarding beyond measure, difficult at times (we do live in a fish bowl of sorts), but I rejoice in our life in the service of the Lord Jesus Christ. When we are doing His will we have peace deep down in our inner beings.

I feel that a clergy wife does not have to fit a particular mold, nor does the clergyman, but that each should follow the bent of her own personality and God-given talents. God will show her the direction of His will when she is open to His leading.

It is extremely important in my estimation that she feel called by the Lord, along with her husband, or she will have a rough row to hoe, and will likely have some difficult time understanding and fitting in with his priorities.

Shark and I belong first to the Lord and then to each other. We are a team.

Years ago someone gave me a delightful clipping from a paper. On it there is pictured a caricature of a woman with descriptive phrases on the sides of the drawing point to various parts of the drawing. It is titled:

"Blueprint for the Ideal Preacher's Wife"

"Radar mind–to know exactly where to reach husband at all times. Automatic mind–to produce Bible school lessons, youth lessons, assisted ladies group devotions, parties, socials, and clever ideas to keep up husband morale. Escape valve–to relieve tensions. Hair–half in fashion of the day, other half motherly style. File cabinet mind–1. Miscellaneous file of all information that husband is apt to forget. 2. Recipe file of 999 ways to prepare hamburger. 3. Information on child psychology, marriage problems, etc. Ear with automatic sifter to sort out information to be repeated from that which is to be kept confidential. One eye in front–for playing the piano, one eye in back–to see what her children are doing in the front pew. Mouth always smiling and saying good things. Four arms–to keep a neat, clean house at all times, keep family neat and well-dressed, do all church work required, raise children to be intelligent and obedient. Figure–not too glamorous and not too matronly. Body – tireless. Clothing–always neat, not too new, not too old, not too fancy, not too plain. Substantial feet - to work and work and work. Available only with ideal preacher. We do not break a set." (Written by C. Boden.)

On June 27, 1960, my husband became the Reverend William Lawrence Sharkey at St. Francis Church in Norris, the mission from which we had gone to seminary. Hank's father presented Shark for ordination and of course Mita was there and Hank and Faye and all our friends who could get there. Bill Pollard preached the ordination sermon and our eldest son, Chip, was the crucifer, he carried the cross in procession.

A touching part of Bill's sermon was his reference to the fact that he and Shark were a little alike in that the Lord had tapped them each on the shoulder and had called them to work for Him. Dr. Pollard pursued his work as a nuclear physicist as well as serving in various churches. It was a glorious festive occasion and we were all

He Gives Us Hope

elated.

We returned from the ordination to get ready for our move to our first church.

Sadly, our dog Pepper was not able to go with us. He had served the family well as both pet and guardian for many years. On one memorable day in Sewanee he had detected a copperhead in the vicinity where the children were playing, had subsequently circled the serpent, barking all the while with an unusual bark, keeping between it and our precious children until Chip alerted his father and Shark arrived and killed the snake. There were extra portions for Pepper that night and many hugs and pats as well as thanksgiving for the children's safety.

Pepper was old and had developed some maladies. We guessed that another transplantation would have been too much for our beloved Schnauzer and as befitted his regal canine bloodline the vet told us he had died of a coronary thrombosis, not just a plain old heart attack! I used to say that his pedigree was probably longer than mine.

The move into the quaint little rectory in Tracy City was exciting but uneventful.

What a varied life we had in that small town. Along with all the church activities we lived and breathed Boy Scouts, Girl Scouts, Cub Scouts, PTA, county fairs, music lessons and recitals, complete with fluttery nerves and fancy dresses, plus awards for excellence (Lucette won those for memory work).

There were school plays, swimming, and occasional fishing expeditions at Grundy Lakes (Griff adored fishing), bike riding and skating on the nice concrete patio in front of the parish house. In bad weather we used that beautifully functional building which was so handy, being right next door between the rectory and the church, for birthday parties and games of all descriptions, even bike riding inside. It was a marvelous place for Chip to practice his drums, when he invested in a set. He could beat them as loudly as he wished and not disturb any of us at home. Each year a highlight was the New Year's eve party for all the church family where we danced, square danced, ate, had hot chocolate and coffee. Our fun culminated in all of us joining hands in a big circle and singing Auld

Lang Syne, whereupon Shark had appropriate prayers, saying farewell to the old year and ushering in the new one, at the stroke of midnight.

One New Year's eve was especially memorable because of a heart-warming episode that took place.

The temperature had taken a big drop and it was snowing hard. Someone selecting food at the big table saw a face peering in the glass double door at one of the front entrances.

Shark was alerted and because he helped people of all circumstances in town recognized the man as one of the town drunks. He invited old Johnny in out of the cold and offered him some hot chocolate and goodies.

Johnny gratefully filled his plate and cup and then huddled down in a chair in one corner of the room watching the festivities.

At the stroke of midnight, with everyone else holding hands in the huge circle, after we had sung, "Auld Lang Syne," Shark ended his prayer by saying, "And God bless us everyone." From the corner a voice issued forth and old Johnny added, "And God bless you, too, Sonny."

Shark was involved in all kinds of community activities as well as holding services at Christ Church and being a real pastor to his flock.

He started a club for senior citizens which met in the parish house. Some elderly men and ladies in town who were virtually housebound had that monthly event as their only opportunity to socialize with friends outside their own churches. They called our Volkswagen bus the "Senior Bus" and thought we had it just for them. Shark went around and picked up those who had no transportation.

Christ Church had a fine youth group who were active in district activities as well as their own, and Shark and I attended diocesan affairs regularly, going to all the conventions, the women's meetings, and many additional conferences at DuBose.

An enthusiastic group of tennis buffs, who kept up running battles on a private tennis court, afforded Shark regular recreation in his favorite sport. I even played with the men sometimes.

He and some of our other adventurous men originated the

He Gives Us Hope

Wilderness Hiking Camp in the diocese. For us it evolved into a family affair. Shark wore a number of hats at various times: leader, cook's helper, Father "Mediquick," jeep driver, assistant trail guide, administrator of the sacraments and "Daddy." We always had worship services which have their own special beauty in the woods.

Chip was a successful camper, assistant to Charlie and Carl, the cooks, and finally counselor and helper to Herman, the hiking guide.

Lucette started as a camper when she was a little girl, her blonde pigtails bouncing as she loped along keeping up with the best of them on the long arduous hikes. Until the Wilderness Hiking Camp ceased to be she was a faithful member of the staff every year as a counselor when she was old enough.

Griff champed at the bit until he was old enough to be included, and the year they first invited girls to come to the camp I was asked to go along as camp mother to give TLC to the girls and anyone else who needed it. They nicknamed me "Cuddles."

That left Hilary who went with us, when I started and for several years after, as camp "mascot." We all loved it and looked forward every summer to that exciting adventure of life in God's magnificent forests. We knew we would have blisters, downpours, drenchings, and not so welcome poison ivy and chiggers, but we always seemed to forget that they were a part of it until we were confronted with them anew.

The woods are our friends, we feel at home in them, and so our family went on numerous camping trips, sleeping in tents and cooking all our meals on an open fire. What delicious food! The boys did a good bit of caving too with people familiar with the caves in the surrounding area. Lucette's scout troop had fun "overnights" in Grundy Forest near us.

Their most extensive undertaking was an excursion to Washington, D.C. After saving their money all year long and carefully researching the historic spots they wanted to see, planning their itinerary, meals, and so forth, ours and several other carloads of giggly girls and their chaperones took off for the Capital; we camped at Hungry Mother State Park in Virginia to and from our destination and staying in the national Girl Scout Camp while in the

He Gives Us Hope

Washington area.

We toured Washington by day in caravan. Shark left the group to attend the College of Preachers in Washington at Mt. St. Albans near the cathedral and the boys and Hilary went by train to Trenton, New Jersey to visit Shark's parents so I drove our VW bus. It was quite an experience. I know I drove through more than one stop sign or red light to avoid getting lost from the rest of the caravan of cars. I was really scared at times, but we made it.

Back home I was consecutively assistant to the Girl Scout leader and then was the Brownie leader because no one else would do it and I really wanted Hilary to have the experience too.

There was always continuous activity at our house with lots of children milling around and playing with our little brood and our dog and cats. We had obtained another dog who "found us" and was Griff's special pet. His name was Curly because of his tail which curled like that of a pig. The was a "Heinz variety," was lots of fun, and very gentle.

Five o'clock we named the "arsenic hour" when the children and I were all tired. I was especially grateful for "Howdy Doody Time" and cartoons on TV while I rustled up dinner.

In our back yard was a lovely old apple tree which bore three varieties of apples (a former priest had grafted the additional kinds) and was perfect for climbing. When the season was right and the children wanted an apple pie or apple crisp, they would go out and pick enough apples, bringing them in to me with big smiles and the

pleas, "Mommy, would you please make us an apple crisp?" There is nothing quite so good as a fresh off the tree home-made apple crisp right out of the oven. I can taste it now.

I had fun with my children when they were small and thoroughly enjoy them as adults.

He Gives Us Hope

We really had fun once a month at a family oriented square dance club where we ate, danced, and laughed until sides hurt as we were far from being experts in the art of square dancing.

Sewanee was near enough for us to take advantage of the many cultural activities offered by the university community.

It was there that I attended my first art class as an adult taught by the artist-in-residence at Sewanee.

I had taken art classes as a child at the Art Museum in Cincinnati, but had not pursued the field for some unknown reasons. In 1966 at the age of forty-four I took up oil painting as a hobby. It is fascinating and affords me therapy, a hobby that is fun, very personalized gifts, and an outlet for my creativity.

There was an SCHC chapter in Sewanee, then led by Margaret Myers. The meeting place was usually Bairnwick and I was eager participant both there and at Adelynrood our home and conference center in Massachusetts.

One companion, Edna, whom I had met at Bairnwick, lived in nearby Monteagle. Edna Myers Snoke was a wonderful person. She had led a very eventful and fruitful life. As a nurse she had done missionary work in China, had been instrumental in starting the Bryn Mawr School of Nursing, had been head of nurses at Johns Hopkins, and while at the hospital had married Dr. John Snoke.

At the time I met Edna she was in her eighties, was widowed and was living with her sister who was a retired schoolteacher. I loved to visit Edna to "get away" from my busy household and particularly because I enjoyed her company. She was warm, loving, and had a gentle wit. I seemed to have been as much help to her as she was to me because the personalities of Edna and her sister were entirely different and when I came, Edna had the opportunity to spout off too, as I did. We laughed a lot together.

We talked a lot about prayer since we were both Companions in the SCHC and one time when I was discussing a prayer concern Edna told me something I shall never forget. In her gentle, wise way she said, "Connie, stop peeking under the leaves to see how God is coming along."

When you know someone loves you, you can be told something profound and you will hear the message clearly and accept what they say. Such was the case with Edna and me. It really sank in. In fact it changed my prayer life considerably. I did stop peeking for the most part and trusted.

Being very family oriented, we Sharkeys and our friends often initiated spur of the moment hikes and cookouts, taking full advantage of the beauty of the mountain in all seasons.

Ever since Lucette was a little girl she had the desire to go back there to teach first grade and help give those mountain children a good start. After living in Jacksonville, Florida and Nashville, Tennessee with the family, Lucette completed her higher education with high honors at Peabody College for Teachers in Nashville and was able to get a job in Pikeville, Tennessee. Since then she has returned to Tracy City and does indeed teach first grade in one of the schools on the mountain. Hers is a real vocation.

Many of those children have had little or no educational advantages or encouragement. Parental motivation is often lacking and they need all the help they can get. Lucette gives them tender loving care and they dearly love her. Upset little folks sit on her lap, stroke her pretty blonde hair, or just enjoy being near her. She makes cupcakes for them on special occasions and does the utmost to stimulate their interest in learning, particularly trying to get them to enjoy reading.

That portion of the Cumberland plateau and the people there are very dear to our hearts, having lived on that mountain for nine years, three in Sewanee (1957-1960) and six in Tracy City (1960-1966) where Shark was ordained priest on February 7, 1960 in Christ Church.

He Gives Us Hope

Chapter 11
THROUGH DEEP VALLEYS

There exists in the minds of many people the misconception that following Jesus will alleviate all problems.

If anyone thinks that by being a Christian life is going to be all peaches and cream, he is on the wrong track. Life is not like that.

Jesus did not promise us that we would have no troubles. He promised that He would be with us and help us get through them and give us victory over our misfortunes. The victory comes through Him, not our own devises and schemes.

I believe that God allows things to happen to us that we don't like. When we turn to Him we certainly see and feel His mercy, power, and love.

The dilemmas with which we were faced during seminary had been small compared to the valley we had to go through in 1963.

It happened on the afternoon of January 13th. The first snowfall of the year was a good one.

We had given Griff, our younger son, a sled for Christmas and he was very eager to try it out for the first time.

As he donned his snow gear and headed for the door he asked the rest of the family, his sister and brother and his daddy and me if we wanted to go sledding. There were no affirmative answers. Each one of us had something that seemed more pressing at the time.

As nine-year-old Griff went out the door his voice echoed, "I wish someone would go with me."

How those words haunted me for eons after that day. I shall never forget them.

An area had been blocked off for sled riding on a good hill a couple of blocks behind our house and the little fellow joined some of the other neighborhood children for an hour or so at that location.

I don't recall what the other members of the family did at that time, but I remember that I took a nap.

The district youth were having their annual "Feast of Lights" at All Saints Chapel in Sewanee. It is a beautiful service that I looked forward to each year and I knew that I would see lots of friends there and wanted to be at my best and not too tired. That was my excuse, I am ashamed to admit.

The service was to start at 6:00 p.m. and we were to leave the house about five, to get there a little early, as Shark was the District Advisor of the E.Y.C. (Episcopal Young Churchmen).

Somewhere in the vicinity of 3 p.m. we heard a knock on the door. When Shark went to answer it Waldo, a neighbor from across the street, anxiously said that there had been an accident up at the corner and could he please come.

Shark asked Waldo who it was and Waldo said it was Griff! He had been hit by a car.

Shark ran out of the house, not bothering to get a coat and went with Waldo to the scene of the accident where, by that time, an ambulance had arrived and they had put the little boy in it.

Shark rode to the doctor's office in the ambulance after summoning me and I drove our car and met Shark there.

Griff was unconscious but did not look all battered and grisly as the newspaper account made it sound. I was grateful for that as I don't have a terrible mental picture of brokenness and blood and was particularly grateful that we could tell the other children, Chip, Lucette, and Hilary in all honesty that the newspaper article was incorrect. I wish newspapers wouldn't do that.

The children did not see him as they had remained in the house when Shark and I went to the doctor's office.

My husband and I went together. Holding each other's hands and touching the quiet limp body we had a prayer that God would heal our son.

The local doctor's diagnosis was that Griff had probably suffered a fractured skull when he had been hit by an oncoming car. He also had a broken leg. As I said, none of the injuries was obvious to us.

He had evidently decided to come home, after sledding with the other children in the blocked off area, and the hill down toward our street was just too inviting for a nine-year-old boy to pass up. That was our guess.

The only problem was that at the bottom of the hill there were rock posts making it impossible to see into the street from either

He Gives Us Hope

side. The snow had melted and refrozen in the streets so as to make it solid ice.

At the same time, Griff took that final ride down the hill an old man was driving in the direction of our house. He could not stop because of the ice. Mr. B. hit Griff head-on with his car.

Griff never knew what hit him and was rendered unconscious immediately.

At the doctor's office we were advised that Griff should be taken to Chattanooga, sixty miles away, to the children's wing of Erlanger Hospital where competent pediatricians and surgeons would examine and treat him with more equipment and expertise.

We decided that I would ride in the ambulance with an attendant and Griff, and Shark would drive down in our car so that we would have a way back home. Some friends rode with him.

We made arrangements for the other three children Chip (13), Lucette (11), and Hilary (5) to stay with neighbors who were also part of our church family.

We also sent out an SOS prayer request immediately to those who were to be at the Feast of Lights in Sewanee and our parishioners plus a number of clergy friends.

Mary, the attendant who was watching over Griff and ministering to his needs in the ambulance, was a friend of ours and happened to be Griff's den mother in Cub scouts. She loved him dearly. Her oldest son was one of our little boy's best buddies.

Mary's job in that circumstance was a very difficult one which she handled with grace. She later told me she was scared to death because the doctor had informed her that Griff might not make it to the hospital, which fact she hid from me very well.

There was no way I could do anything except sit and watch and pray because, as well as being in a state of shock, I was absolutely uplifted by all the prayers that were being offered by our many concerned loving friends. I felt a calmness that was unbelievable.

One thought kept going through my mind over and over again, "He's going to make it. He's going to make it. He's going to make it."

That is all I could think of and it was very positive and strong.

The sixty miles seemed interminable.

On our arrival at Erlanger Hospital we were met at the emergency entrance and Griff was whisked off to X-ray. Our next glimpse of him was some time later in ICU.

By that time several of our close Chattanooga friends had been alerted and had come to sit out the ordeal with us at the hospital, among them two clergymen Robbie and Harold and one of my SCHC companions, Elizabeth.

We were very grateful for their presence and prayer support.

The doctors confirmed the diagnosis of a broken leg and said that Griff had sustained multiple fractures of the skull plus probable internal injuries. No surgery was suggested.

As I waited and talked to my friend Elizabeth I remember telling her that I would probably have to teach Griff to walk again and I envisioned my darling little boy and I working together toward that goal.

As is the custom in most hospitals, patients can be seen in the Intensive Care Unit for only five minutes every half hour. Shark and I waited all those tortuous minutes in between until we could see our very special little boy and gaze on his silence. We prayed as we watched.

There was no sign of his regaining consciousness.

A nurse told us that he was breathing five times a minute.

My conscious mind took hold of reason long enough for me to realize for the first time, a clue, an inkling, that he would not live.

It was a precious softening of the blow which I am certain our loving God gave me in preparation.

We had another prayer, our last with him in this world. We had to leave again and go into the waiting room.

Shortly thereafter someone called us into another room and I was given a pill and told to sit down. Then they told us that he had died.

It sunk in. There was no disbelief of the fact that he was gone, no denial. We poured out the first tears of grief in the presence of a doctor, some nurses, and our two priest friends, Robbie and Harold. They were so helpful.

Bishop Vander Horst and his wife, Helen, came from a dedication of a new church directly to the hospital to be with my husband

and me. I remember as we walked out of the hospital telling them. "Thank God I have three more children at home." Only by the grace of God could I have been thankful for something at that time.

As we were being driven back home by one of our parishioners I remembered the words that had kept running through my mind, "He's going to make it." I could not understand. Then suddenly the thought came, he did make it. He was with God. He who had shortly before told me, "Mommy, you know who I love more than anyone in the world? God." The little boy who loved everyone, the child who had chosen and bought a plaque at school on which the words were, "The gift of God is Eternal Life" had hung it over his bed. He knew God and believed, so I know where he has been ever since. I have someone on the other side praying for me. And I have others too.

Something happened that day to the girl who rode in the ambulance with me. She told me later that her life changed. I don't know in what way, but God had touched her. He was with us.

When we arrived home from the hospital and walked into our living room, about half the people from our little church where Shark was the priest were waiting for us, offering their love in a variety of ways. We needed their presence so badly. Our children had been told.

I will take the liberty to say here that if any of you readers are ever in a predicament and have no idea what to say or do for someone who is bereaved, just do or say what comes naturally to you. It might be a squeeze of a hand or a hug. Or say how much the person meant to you.

There is no correct answer in my book. Whatever each friend expressed to me was just right for them. Their love and concern came through right then, in our living room, and for days afterwards.

A note might suit your temperament and abilities. Some people quoted Bible verses or told us something that was very helpful to them when they went through a valley of sorrow. I still have some of the letters that were sent to us, they were so beautiful. Powerful support comes through the pen of those who express their love in that manner.

Food arrived and people to serve it. Many brought casseroles, cakes, salads, and soup was a favorite. It is easy to digest and very comforting when one is tired.

One person took soiled linens and clothes from the hampers and brought them back clean. Others vacuumed and dusted the house. One man unobtrusively stoked the furnace for days for Shark.

It is very difficult to think in a normal way when grief stricken.

My very dear and wise friend Mita even came and took me home to her house to get a nap, away from everything else. I had not realized I was tired. She had been through it many years before. She knew.

Her son Hank, our former priest, flew in from his home in Connecticut to be with us and help with the necessary arrangements.

"Griffie," as I often called our youngest son, and I were very close. He was named for me. My name is Mary Constance Griffith Sharkey. His name is Conrad Griffith Sharkey. He even looked quite a bit like me in that our faces were shaped alike and we both had blonde hair and blue eyes.

When he was a little fellow and had started to nursery school he cried and cried every day, not wanting to go.

One day I asked him what was wrong, thinking that he might be having some psychological problem with the teacher or some other children and he said, "I just want to be with you, Mommy." I melted and gave him a huge hug and a kiss.

With that knowledge and our love for each other he got over the hump and went on to nursery school and in time adjusted to it.

After his death I was given the fortitude to wash and iron his Cub Scout uniform for his burial.

His body lay in state in our beautiful little church with always two people keeping the vigil night and day. Those who came to see us went first to the church, two doors away, to be with God, then came to our home where we received them.

I recall feeling so sorry for some of them because they were so overcome and didn't know what to do or say. I could never have been concerned for them and prayed for them had not God been with me. In fact the Methodist minister's wife remarked to me,

"You are with God aren't you Connie?"

I said, "Yes." We both knew it.

When friends came to have a visit with me I really appreciated their being open and talking about him, remembering the fun things that Griff did and the very special traits that gave him warmth and his unique personality. He was a very special little boy. Their being natural was the most help of all.

Griff's dog Curly sat on the front steps of the church the whole time until the funeral. We were all amazed. He wouldn't come home.

One day the old man who had been driving the car came with two of his adult children to see us. He was extremely upset and contrite.

We told him that we didn't believe that anyone would hit a little boy on purpose.

The three of them were very relieved and grateful and one of Mr. Brown's sons said, "You are certainly people of God."

Mr. Brown then revealed something that was very gratifying to us. He said that he had seen Griff coming down the hill, lickety split, with a grin from ear to ear. He was having a ball.

It meant so much to me because I knew he had been having a good time and was evidently not aware of or frightened by the oncoming disaster. He never knew what hit him and probably did not see the car because the rock posts obscured the view from both directions.

Later when Mr. Brown was in the hospital in Sewanee, Shark went to see him a number of times. Shark felt that the old gentleman died of a broken heart, along with whatever illness plagued him.

We cried the most at night, by ourselves, in bed, Shark and I.

Had our child lived he would likely have been paralyzed and had brain damage.

We knew that he had been undergirded by prayer and God's loving kindness and so had we. We had felt comfort, love, and grace that pass all understanding.

We were grateful that he was free and with God though we missed him terribly. He had loved life so fully and had derived so much from it. He was like a little St. Francis. Griff loved everyone and everyone loved him. He was gentle, kind, beautiful, sensitive, and friendly.

One time he asked me why some people were mean and I had told him I really didn't know why, they just were. He could not understand it. (I know now that sometimes people were mean to him.)

His funeral was beautiful. It was a glorious tribute to the living risen Christ. Easter hymns were sung. Everyone received the Eucharist.

There were so many people that one of our parishioners had set up a P.A. system in the parish hall to accommodate the overflow so that everyone who had come could hear and take part in the service.

There were times when I would begin to sob at which times my Companion friends who were sitting directly behind me, looking out for me, shot up prayers to God. I felt them instantly and was calmed. At the end of the service the organist played on the bells "Christ the Lord is Risen Today" and that glorious hymn was heard all over town.

Monks were there, our Bishops, John Vander Horst and Bill and Kitty Sanders, and other friends came from miles away to be with us. It was God's love in action, given directly to us and through others, an outpouring.

Little children are very perceptive and can be utterly profound. Our youngest child, Hilary, was only five at the time and she said one day, "You know what Mommy, when I feel close to God I feel close to Griff." I think that is beautiful! To me it is "the communion of saints" in a nutshell. We are separated from our loved ones only in the physical sense. In our hearts we are still together and always will be.

I do not think that God caused that accident as some people seemed to think and intimated to us. I think He allowed it to happen. I think the accident was the result of human error on the part of at least three people, one of them being me. Griff had been told to stay off the street. Though the street where he started was blocked off for sledding and therefore safe, the ones where he was hit had not been blocked off and were therefore unsafe. An old man was

He Gives Us Hope

driving on ice, a condition where one cannot be in control of an automobile. I did not honor my son's request when he said, "I wish someone would go with me."

We are not puppets dangling on strings. God has always allowed us the precious freedom of choice. We make some decisions that are good and some that are bad. When we turn to Him and ask His guidance and follow it, I know God honors our obedience. When we disregard Him and make false choices and later turn to Him with penitent and contrite hearts He forgives us and redeems us. God is glorified.

In the case of that terrible accident many prayers had been offered. God heard those prayers and answered them. He overcame all the bad with His goodness and loving kindness.

Our dear son who had been so badly hurt was taken out of his brokenness by Almighty God into His safe keeping and given the precious gift of Eternal Life. God gave comfort and strength to our whole family and increased the trust and faith of all who shared in the experience.

One of the difficult jobs with which we were faced was to go through Griff's clothes and do something with them.

He and Chip shared a room and it was not fair for Griff's things to still be there when he himself was not there, and never coming back.

It was particularly necessary for me to do that job because after Sally died the task had been done for me by Shark and our friends

 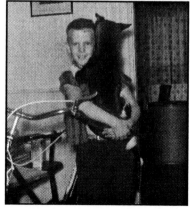

to spare me more grief. They were trying to help. But that is part of the grief process. It helps one work through feelings that need to be dealt with.

A very jolting awareness occurred to me for some time when I would automatically call Griff to get up, or come to meals or prepare to tell him goodnight and expect him to be there. We establish such habits that it takes quite some time for them to be broken. We know in our minds that the loved one is gone but we cannot fully grasp that reality for a while. Each time the reality sinks in from the jolt we become more accepting.

I was lifted up and being carried by grace. That is the only way I can describe my feeling. I know the prayers of many friends were sustaining me and God was dealing with me in the time frame He knew I could handle.

Emotional shock seems to affect people on a very individual basis. There is no set pattern or time frame.

I thought of all the happy times we had together, of all the loving aspects of Griff's life and personality.

He loved to fish and I could picture him happily fishing in the "ocean of God's love."

I am so pleased to say that our family has always talked about Griff freely and all of his part of our family activities. He was a very integral part of us for nine and a half years.

We continue to include him naturally in our reminiscences. We remember the good and the not so good things about him, little idiosyncracies as well as his loving qualities. We laugh at his foibles and mistakes the same as we do the other members of our family.

After a death those remaining tend to idolize the deceased. The time has to come when we remember them as they really are, imperfect but lovable human beings, children of God, and members of our families.

After about three months a friend called me one day from Sewanee and asked how I was doing. I hesitated for a moment and then said, in all honestly, that the cookie had crumbled!

The terrible guilt I felt for the fact that I had not gone with Griff surfaced. It was awful. I was tormented. I faced it fully and directly.

I told the Lord all about it and He in His mercy gave me His forgiveness completely, absolutely. Forgiveness is glorious!

He made me a new creature. I was free of the chains that had bound me.

Then God began to use the new butterfly I had become in beautiful and unexpected ways. I was able to help others who faced similar tragedies.

I talked about it a good bit and particularly how the Lord had helped me.

A strange statement emerged from my heart and mouth. I told people it was the worst experience I had ever had and also one of the most beautiful. That referred to God's part in it and how He showered His love on all of us directly and through His body, the Church.

When I told the story to others it seemed to help not only them but me. Then I began feeling that I was dwelling on it too much, and the opportunity arose for me to attend a Churchwomen's conference at DuBose.

While I was there I made my confession that I felt that I was talking about me too much.

The answer the Lord told me was unmistakable and startling.

He said in no uncertain terms, "This is not yours to cherish, it is yours to share."

Since that moment I have not been hesitant. Whenever appropriate times occur, and they are not difficult to discern, in fact the Lord brings them to my awareness, I relate the story to the glory of God.

God is eternal, God is timeless. God's forgiveness is glorious. I know that my redeemer liveth. I know for sure that He was resurrected and that we will be too. I know that He gives us the Life abundant on this earth as well as in the life to come.

"Nay in all these things we are more than conquerors through Him that loved us. For I am persuaded, that neither death, nor life, nor angels, nor principalities, nor powers, nor things present, nor things to come, nor height, nor depth, nor any other creature, shall be able to separate us from the love of God, which is in Christ Jesus our Lord" (Romans 8:37-39 KJV).

Chapter 12
IT'S HARD TO LET GO

Why is it that we seem to have to face some of our most difficult decisions in the wake of suffering a terrible blow?

I am not sure of the answer to that question, but I do know that one such predicament presented itself to us in the spring after Griff's fatal accident. The outcome of that decision opened the door for me to a beautiful sequence of interaction and growth, the knowledge of which has been invaluable to me many times since then.

Chip was finishing the eighth grade and showed promise of exceptional ability. Naturally, as parents, we felt that he had talent, but our feelings were reinforced by the fact that two of his teachers came to us individually and told Shark and me virtually the same thing, and wondered if we were aware of our son's capabilities and hoped that we would offer him the opportunity to develop his potential.

St. Andrews school was not far away. It was an excellent boy's school run by the Episcopal monks of the Order of the Holy Cross, offering well-rounded education designed to develop the whole person, in body, mind, and spirit.

Since it was only about ten miles away we were well aware of its existence and knew a number of men in town who had gone there and who praised it highly.

Chip had become interested in St. Andrews and had mentioned the fact that he would like to go there but with all the trauma of the death of our younger son we were not thinking in that direction.

The accident had been in January. Late that spring Chip came to us one day and asked if he might go to St. Andrews in the fall. We were temporarily stunned. Our first human reaction was that we could not let him go. Griff's loss was so great that we were holding on for dear life to our remaining three children. Those of us who have lost dear ones know the feeling. We want instinctively to protect and hover over the others so that nothing will happen to them. I think the reaction is very normal.

On further thought we remembered that the local county high

He Gives Us Hope

school was not geared to being college preparatory because a very small percentage of students graduating from there pursued higher education. Those who did, usually fared quite well because of their ability and determination.

We were caught in a dilemma. We absolutely had to think about Chip and not ourselves.

Then we thought of the girls. Having lost one brother so suddenly, we felt that it would be terrible to have both of them gone, but we decided to talk to them about it and get their reactions. Lucette was then eleven and Hilary was six years old. Lucette had been especially close to Griff.

We asked them how they would feel if Chip could get a scholarship and go to St. Andrews in the fall. We had in the meantime learned that financial aid was possible and available (we could never have afforded it otherwise), and he would have to be a boarding student in order to reap the greatest possible benefits from the rich curriculum offered.

Bless their hearts, they both said that they thought it would be great! We were both amazed and pleased.

Then as Shark and I shared our feelings further we felt that if the girls could accept it so beautifully we could not be selfish and possessive but should let him go. His whole future seemed to depend on it.

We told Chip "Yes" and proceeded to make the preliminary arrangements for his entrance in September.

Making the initial decision was the hardest part, but it took all the courage we could muster, upheld by the prayers of many, for us to take our dear son to St. Andrews at the beginning of the school year, knowing that for his good we were not to visit him for the first six weeks, nor would he be permitted to come home for visits after that, except some Sunday afternoons, until the Thanksgiving holidays and later Christmas. It was extremely difficult, but by the grace of God we did it.

Our reward came the first time we saw him, six weeks later. All we had to do was take one look at his face and see that he was radiantly happy, to know for sure that we had done the right thing.

His four years there were all we could have hoped for plus a hundredfold more. He excelled in his studies, receiving yearly awards in many subjects. He participate fully in the spiritual life, so important to the St. Andrews family. He was assigned as head prefect of his dorm his senior year and was valedictorian of his graduating class.

Chip and his roommate, Haynes, who was an outstanding athlete, had helped each other reciprocally with the areas in which each was least proficient. On the wall of the refectory is a plaque naming the top student and top athlete of each class. Chip's and Haynes Wilkes' names are there for posterity.

Our son wrestled, played tennis and then was asked to be the manager of the football team, which activity and training preceded and subsequently afforded him the opportunity of obtaining a four-year working scholarship as a football manager at the University of Florida, his alma mater.

In the ensuing years I have known the necessity of letting go of each of our children in turn. It is never easy, but that very positive action seems to be imperative for their being able to blossom fully. As long as we who are parents hang on to our children and try to decide what we think should be their futures we can easily stunt their growth, or worse still we might lead them in a direction contrary to that which only our heavenly Father knows to be their true vocations.

He knows their strengths and weaknesses, their inherent talents and the extent to which they as children of God can develop.

He knows all about each of us, even the number of hairs on our heads. Our responsibility and privilege is to trust Him, to "let go and let God."

A beautiful prayer in our Prayer Book helps me when I reach that point of having to let any loved one go, be it child, husband or friend. The prayer is under the heading, "For Those We Love" and it reads: "Almighty God, we entrust all who are dear to us to thy never-failing care and love, for this life and the life to come; knowing that thou art doing for them better things than we can desire or pray for; through Jesus Christ our Lord. Amen" (1979 BCP, p. 831).

The last facet of letting go, or better still the first, is of ourselves. If we really want to be who we are meant to be we put our

He Gives Us Hope

hearts, our souls, our minds, and our bodies, every fibre of our being in His care. He will lead us in His way. We will be at peace.

In the practice of intercessory prayer, letting go and letting God is equally important when one is confronted with a real dilemma.

I can remember one such instance way back in Norris. No man-made solution seemed adequate, practical, or feasible for a problem that my friend Dorothy and I were praying about. We were really in the soup!

I recall that we finally gave up and turned the whole thing over to God. Some days later Dorothy called me utterly amazed and thrilled about what had happened to the complex problem and we laughed wholeheartedly when she remarked, "I could never have thought of that." We agreed that God is a lot smarter than we are.

He Gives Us Hope

Chapter 13
THANKSGIVING IS MORE THAN A DAY
TO AT TURKEY

I often get my inspirations for my writing when I am doing the simple jobs such as cooking, cleaning, pulling weeds, cutting the grass, or even sewing or ironing. We look for God in big things and He surprises us with His presence in little things, the ordinary. I am an artist and He quite often speaks to me when I paint, as I almost always pray before I paint.

I have found, too, that offering whatever mundane job I have to do as intercession for someone I'm concerned about is one beneficial way to pray. It has transformed housework for me from boring chores to occasions of purpose and even fun. I certainly cannot take credit for the idea.

I first became aware of it when I heard about Brother Lawrence, that glorious 17th century monk who cleaned pots and pans in a monastery kitchen to the glory of God and found heaven on earth.

To quote a portion of the preface of the original French edition 1692 A.D., of "The Practice of the Presence of God": "All, whatever their life work, will find profit, for they will see here in a brother . . . who was in the midst of the most exacting occupations has learnt so well to accord action with contemplation, that for the space of more than forty years he hardly ever turned from the presence of God."

I used to really dislike cutting the grass. One particular day I decided to cut the front yard to the glory of God with special intention for my friend Anne. She was going through a trying time with one of her children's heartaches. It took me a lot less time than usual to cut the grass, it seemed, and I really didn't mind doing it. Later that day Anne called to tell me that something very exciting had happened, a sort of "breakthrough" for the child she was concerned about and she wanted to share the good news with me. Then I told her about the grass and the prayer. We both praised the Lord. Things do happen when we pray.

One young lady heard me telling that story one day to a group of people and asked what cutting the grass had to do with the particular problem that Anne and I were praying for. She was one of those persons who are always trying to discern hidden meaning and connections in everything. I answered her, rather startled and somewhat irritated, "Not a darned thing. I needed to cut the grass and they had a problem we were praying about. God used my prayers for His purposes." We don't have to know why or how. Maybe I wasn't too nice, but I felt she was trying to complicate things.

One morning I was fixing turkey for a friend of mine who had undergone surgery. As I prayed for Linda, and I did the work a la Brother Lawrence, I thought of Thanksgiving.

Thanksgiving is the time our family usually has turkey. I fix it often during the year in addition to Thanksgiving because we not only love roast turkey, dressing, and gravy but we really relish all the goodies that come after the first feast: sandwiches, turkey casserole or hash, creamed turkey on waffles, and last but not least the delicious homemade turkey soup from the bones and skin. (Besides it is very economical.) So often the raw materials of our needs are right under our noses. I did have a turkey on hand.

I was very grateful that I knew that it was one of Linda's favorite foods because I really wanted to do something special for her and her family, particularly when she was in need. I liked the entire family, they were members of our church and through their generosity I was afforded the special treat of frequent swims in their private pool. So that she would not have to even think about the evening meal, I called to let her know that I would bring dinner over for her and her family.

I had a good time preparing it and I began giving thanks as I worked. When we give thanks, floodgates of God's graces are opened.

Robert Raynolds, in his beautiful book, "In Praise of Gratitude" (Harper and Bros., 1961), has innumerable statements about gratitude, but one of my favorites is, "Gratitude is our living harmony with the music of God."

If you are ever disgruntled try giving thanks for anything. You may have to start with something very simple. When I am down in the dumps and have lots of work facing me and really don't feel like doing it, I have found that if I give thanks for any one thing, no matter how small, my attitude will change. In obedience I begin that chore as I give thanks.

For instance, if I have mounds of wash to do I start out with something like, "Thank you Lord that I have a washing machine, and it works." Then, "Thank you Lord, that my family and I have clothes to wear. Thank You that I have time available to prepare them for the family's use. Thank You that I have a husband who loves me and provides for me and that we have beautiful children. Thank You that I have eyes to see what I am doing. Thank You that I have ears to hear the birds when I hang the clothes outside and for the sun and wind and fresh air in which to dry them and when the weather is bad that I have a dryer inside in which to dry them. Thank You that I have healthy limbs. Thank You that I have a heart and soul to respond to You."

Gratitude grows and grows and grows, and one is no longer down in the dumps but lifted up to Him, the Creator and Giver of all good gifts.

You know God must be pleased when we give Him thanks. We certainly like having our children thank us for gifts we have given them, and I feel sure in my heart that thanksgiving pleases our Heavenly Father.

Most of us enjoy doing things for people we love. I love God because He has been so good to me, given me so much and my desire is to do His will.

I turn often to Him to find out what He would have me do. It is not always easy, in fact at times following His leading is very difficult, but it always pays off.

I have found that God usually directs individuals in ways that use the talents and skills they already have. He is very practical. But there are times when He asks us to perform tasks for which we feel inadequate. That is all the better. At those times we must depend on Him absolutely because we know we are incapable of accomplishing the tasks on our own. When it is His work He will provide the wisdom, skill, and power necessary. With the call comes the provision.

He Gives Us Hope

The Bible is full of accounts of God's people who did what He asked them to do, even when they did not understand why. He requested and they responded. We have the freedom of choice to say "No." That precious freedom insures that we are not puppets.

Ponder the lives of Noah, Moses, Isaac, the disciples Jesus called to follow Him, and Paul and Ananias; the man Jesus told to go and wash in the pool of Siloam, the man He told to pick up his mat and go home. Blessed Mary said "yes" to God and brought Jesus into the human scene, then He, the one perfect person freely gave His life for you, me, and all mankind. The world has never been the same. Praise God.

If we say "Yes" to God it won't change the world, but it may change our lives and possibly the lives of those close to us.

If you get a prompting to call, write, or visit a friend, or make a dinner for someone who is sick, try to follow it up. Find out what it is like. It is exciting!

For years I have had a desire to write a book. That hope has come to fruition, with His help.

In 1963, after Griff's death, the Lord told me to write. I have been doing so off and on ever since. It is, at this writing, the Year of our Lord 1992 and I have the joy of sharing with you the Hope that only He can give. Thanks be to God.

EPILOGUE

Our life in the ministry for over forty years has been very rewarding. Both Shark and I have really enjoyed it and all the people we have been privileged to know. We have been in a number of locations, all very diverse, and each with its own uniqueness.

As you have read in "HE GIVES US HOPE," we started out in Tracy City, Tennessee. We were there from 1960 to 1966, and from that mountain community we went for two and a half years to a church that was really hurting because their rector had left the ministry. That particular church, the Church of the Epiphany, a beautiful modern looking building, was located between two Naval air stations in Jacksonville, Florida, and had a congregation composed of mostly military personnel and their families. We did our best to provide healing and cohesiveness for them. While we were living in Jacksonville, both of my parents died in Cincinnati. In 1969, Shark's parents were getting along in years and having some physical problems so we felt we should be farther north to be close to them, plus we were homesick for Tennessee.

The Bishop of Tennessee called Shark and told him that there was a church in Nashville that really needed him; their rector had been killed in an automobile accident. Because the need was urgent, we felt the wisest course of action was to move up there early in the year and leave Lucette, who was a senior in high school, to live with friends in Jacksonville until she graduated in June. That decision was made after much prayer and deliberation. We were at St. Matthias in Nashville from 1969 to 1975. Nana Sharkey, after a period of time in a nursing home, died in Trenton while we were living in Nashville. Pop came to live with us for four years before he passed on, while in a nursing home in nearby Chattanooga.

Since we always pray diligently when Shark receives a call, to discern if that is where the Lord really wants us, we had a rather difficult decision with one particular call. In 1975 the Bishop of Missouri, who had known Shark well and had worked with him in Tennessee, asked us to come to Sikeston, Missouri. That was "flat-

He Gives Us Hope

land" and we would be away from Tennessee and our children, but we really felt certain that the Lord wanted us to go there so we went. It was a wonderful five years (from 1975 to 1980) with a lovely congregation, a beautiful colonial style church. We really enjoyed our stay there, as we have each place we have ministered, finding that every congregation has its special needs and particular joys. We know for sure that when we are called by the Lord to a place, and we depend on Him continually for guidance, our ministry prospers and the church and its members learn more of His goodness, loving kindness, and the power of His forgiveness. We can absolutely depend on Him at all times. That proved to be so at St. Paul's, Sikeston, Missouri.

Following our stay in Sikeston, we moved back to Tennessee, that time to Memphis, to another St. Paul's. That congregation was struggling because of plant closings in the area. Again we had a good experience for a period of three years.

Then, in a most unusual sequence of events, we were called to Shark's next cure. He was led to take early retirement at age 62 and to go to Christ Church, Cedar Key, Florida (which is located on the west coast of Florida, halfway between Tallahassee and Tampa, not in the "keys" as many people think), in August 1984, as a retired priest, employed to work three days a week. In this location, he was virtually free of pollen induced allergies, which was a tremendous blessing. The last three rectories in which we lived, we had electro-static filters installed on our heating-air conditioning systems to reduce the effects of his allergies. Shark fell in love with the place the first time he drove on to the island. He loved islands anyway, (shades of his early years on Great Chebeague island in Casco Bay, Maine, where he spent summers with his grandmother); and even more wonderful was the fact that he could suddenly breathe so much more freely. God is so good!

It is amazing how the Lord has used us in such differing environments, and He has given us rich blessings in every church and town or city where He has brought us. He has always taken care of us and we have had everything we have really needed.

If you would ask us how we managed to put three children through college on what he has made (most of the churches being fairly small and so with not too much money), we could not tell you except for the fact that our children worked hard, had some jobs and scholarship assistance, and we contributed the best we could, and all in all, by the grace of God.

Chip graduated from the University of Florida with the first degree that they awarded in Commercial Recreation. He worked for the "theme parks" Opryland in Nashville and Busch Gardens in Williamsburg, VA. While working, he attended American University on weekends and earned a Masters Degree in Human Resource Development. He is presently Senior Vice President, Human Resources at Direct Holdings Worldwide LLC, the parent company of Lillian Vernon Corporation and Time-Life. He lives in Surry, VA, is married to Joann and has three step-children and five grandchildren.

Lucette earned a B.S. in Elementary Education from the George Peabody College for Teachers in Nashville, enabling her to fulfill her childhood dream of returning to the Cumberland Plateau to teach first grade and help those little children get a good start. She lives in Tracy City, where she is a member of our former church, Christ Church, and is a very valued resident of her community.

Hilary has a B.A. in Interior Design from Lambuth University in Jackson, TN. She now has her own interior design business in Nashville. Her specialty is hospitality (hotel) design but she also does residential and commercial work. She was a member of the design team that developed the Homewood Suites brand of extended-stay hotels.

They are all three wonderful children, very loving to us and to so many others. They are responsible, hardworking, caring and giving, very involved in their respective churches and communities. Beautiful Christians of whom we are very proud. We are indeed blessed beyond measure. They are lots of fun, too.

Shark and I moved back to Nashville in 1994 to be closer to our girls, and since we are getting older, also to be nearer doctors and hospitals for our medical needs. Shark still does some supply work in the Diocese of Tennessee and has been the interim rector at several churches in Nashville, as well as the chaplain to the retired clergy, spouses, widows and widowers in the diocese. He loves to stay

He Gives Us Hope

busy. The good Lord has blessed our marriage for 59 years, as of this writing.

On May 31, 2003, Shark died of lung cancer. After a very full life, at age 81, he was "promoted to glory." At his request, this triumphant phrase is engraved on his tombstone in Tracy City.

Printed in the United States
20359LVS00002B/751-774

9 780975 564653